D0885785

Slavery

Thomas Streissguth, *Book Editor*

Bonnie Szumski, *Editorial Director*
Scott Barbour, *Managing Editor*
David M. Haugen, *Series Editor*

Greenhaven Press, Inc., San Diego, California

Library of Congress Cataloging-in-Publication Data

Slavery / Thomas Streissguth, book editor.
    p. cm. — (History firsthand)
    Includes bibliographical references (p.) and index.
    ISBN 0-7377-0633-3 (lib. bdg. : alk. paper) —
    ISBN 0-7377-0632-5 (pbk. : alk. paper)
    1. Slavery—United States—History—Sources. 2. Slaves—
United States—Social conditions—Sources. 3. Slaves—United
States—Biography. 4. Slaveholders—United States—Biography.
I. Streissguth, Thomas, 1958–   . II. Series.

E441 .S617 2001
306.3'62—dc21   2001016034

Cover photo: Picture Quest/Michael Brady
Library of Congress, 121
North Wind Picture Archives, 11, 143

Contents

Chapter 1: The Slave Trade

1. A Voyage to West Africa
The profitable slave trade drew many ambitious colonials to Atlantic port cities, where slave merchants hired out ship officers as well as ordinary sailors. A Charleston gentleman joins a slaving expedition to West Africa, where he encounters the trade's customary evils and comes to regret his choice of career.

2. The Middle Passage
Millions of African captives were packed and transported like cattle across the Atlantic Ocean during the harrowing Middle Passage. An eighteenth-century survivor of the voyage recounts his capture and experience aboard a slaving ship.

3. A Day at the Slave Auctions
The trade in human beings seemed worthy of investigation by many European visitors to North America. A gentleman from Scotland spends a day strolling and browsing through the slave-selling district of Richmond, Virginia.

Chapter 2: Foreign Perspectives

1. A Redcoat's View of Plantation Life
By the time of the American Revolution, slave labor formed an economic mainstay for the Chesapeake region, a center of the tobacco trade. A British prisoner

of war observes slavery firsthand while being marched through Maryland and Virginia.

Chapter 3: A Life in Bondage

traders and owners. A slave owner in debt must decide whether to sell his favorite property—a loyal and hardworking slave.

writer also insists on the beneficial social and economic influences of the South's "peculiar institution."

Foreword

In his preface to a book on the events leading to the Civil War, Stephen B. Oates, the historian and biographer of Abraham Lincoln, John Brown, and other noteworthy American historical figures, explained the difficulty of writing history in the traditional third-person voice of the biographer and historian. "The trouble, I realized, was the detached third-person voice," wrote Oates. "It seemed to wring all the life out of my characters and the antebellum era." Indeed, how can a historian, even one as prominent as Oates, compete with the eloquent voices of Daniel Webster, Abraham Lincoln, Harriet Beecher Stowe, Frederick Douglass, and Robert E. Lee?

Oates's comment notwithstanding, every student of history, professional and amateur alike, can name a score of excellent accounts written in the traditional third-person voice of the historian that bring to life an event or an era and the people who lived through it. In *Battle Cry of Freedom*, James M. McPherson vividly re-creates the American Civil War. Barbara Tuchman's *The Guns of August* captures in sharp detail the tensions in Europe that led to the outbreak of World War I. Taylor Branch's *Parting the Waters* provides a detailed and dramatic account of the American Civil Rights Movement. The study of history would be impossible without such guiding texts.

Nonetheless, Oates's comment makes a compelling point. Often the most convincing tellers of history are those who lived through the event, the eyewitnesses who recorded their firsthand experiences in autobiographies, speeches, memoirs, journals, and letters. The Greenhaven Press History Firsthand series presents history through the words of first-person narrators. Each text in this series captures a significant historical era or event—the American Civil War, the

Great Depression, the Holocaust, the Roaring Twenties, the 1960s, the Vietnam War. Readers will investigate these historical eras and events by examining primary-source documents, authored by chroniclers both famous and little known. The texts in the History Firsthand series comprise the celebrated and familiar words of the presidents, generals, and famous men and women of letters who recorded their impressions for posterity, as well as the statements of the ordinary people who struggled to understand the storm of events around them—the foot soldiers who fought the great battles and their loved ones back home, the men and women who waited on the breadlines, the college students who marched in protest.

The texts in this series are particularly suited to students beginning serious historical study. By examining these firsthand documents, novice historians can begin to form their own insights and conclusions about the historical era or event under investigation. To aid the student in that process, the texts in the History Firsthand series include introductions that provide an overview of the era or event, timelines, and bibliographies that point the serious student toward key historical works for further study.

The study of history commences with an examination of words—the testimony of witnesses who lived through an era or event and left for future generations the task of making sense of their accounts. The Greenhaven Press History Firsthand series invites the beginner historian to commence the process of historical investigation by focusing on the words of those individuals who made history by living through it and recording their experiences firsthand.

Introduction

A frican slavery in the Western Hemisphere began in the sixteenth century, when captives were first brought across the Atlantic from the western coasts of Africa to work on European sugar plantations in Cuba, Jamaica, Barbados, Antigua, and several other Caribbean islands. During the next three centuries, two-thirds of all slaves in the New World lived and died on Caribbean sugar plantations. The cutting and burning of sugarcane was one of the most exhausting and dangerous forms of slavery. Harsh work and rampant disease cut short the lives of most Caribbean slaves; meanwhile, their owners lived elsewhere and left the care and management of plantation laborers in the hands of overseers.

A very different form of slavery evolved on the North American mainland. Accustomed to considering land as private property, to be claimed, cleared, and planted for profit, European settlers faced a difficult challenge in taming the immense stretch of uncultivated land along the Atlantic seaboard. The hungry European market for rice, sugar, and tobacco could not be satisfied without laborers to work this new land, and at first very little labor was available.

To provide the needed workers, some landowners captured Native Americans. Their efforts failed, however, as North American Indians could not adapt to either farming or slavery. Most Indian men still lived by hunting and gathering and fiercely resisted farmwork, considering it unmanly and demeaning. With their knowledge of the surrounding hills and forests, the Indians also found it easy to escape their would-be owners and disappear into the wilderness. The settlers faced the problem of dwindling supply: by the end of the seventeenth century, warfare and disease were destroying the eastern tribes and driving the survivors west, into the interior, and for the time being, far from European settlement.

A better solution for the labor shortage arrived with European indentured servants, who were given free passage to America in exchange for a few years of their labor. (Other indentured servants worked in bondage for the settlement of a debt or to serve a term of punishment handed down by a judge.) Hard economic times in England in the mid–seventeenth century prompted many of the poor and unemployed to sign themselves into this temporary slavery in the hopes of eventually attaining their own land and property in North America. But until they were freed, indentured servants had few legal rights. They were under the mastery of those who had bought their services and who could inflict punishment as they saw fit. During a term of service, indentured servants could also be bought and sold by their owners like any other personal property.

By the end of the seventeenth century, England was recovering from a civil war and an economic depression. The improving conditions in England allowed wages for laborers to rise in the mother country, and as a result, fewer people were selling themselves into indentured servitude in the colonies. Yet the demand for cash crops such as tobacco, indigo, sugar, and rice continued to be strong in European markets, and America was becoming an essential supplier of such crops. To keep their estates productive, American landowners turned to a new source of labor: African slaves.

African Slavery in the Colonies

The continent's first such slaves had arrived in 1619, sold in Jamestown, Virginia, by a Dutch merchant captain. But through the rest of the century, as indentured servants arrived to make up a large portion of the unskilled labor force, the demand for African slaves remained low. Africans were utterly foreign to the British colonists; they did not speak English or any other European language, understand Europe's customs of dress and behavior, or believe in the Christian religion. They were not adapted to the climate and had little resistance to European diseases. Breaking Africans into slavery on a tobacco or rice plantation was difficult and time-consuming, and their transportation across the Atlantic made them more expensive than white indentured servants.

This situation changed in the late seventeenth century. New laws in the North American colonies—such as a law that barred freedom for slaves who converted to Christianity—made it easier for planters to keep African slaves. In addition, the powerful English navy was allowing English merchants to muscle in on the African slave trade, which had been previously dominated by the Dutch. The easier trade in slaves allowed their prices to fall while the area under cultivation in the colonies was increasing rapidly. A busy market in bonded human laborers developed along North America's Atlantic coast.

The slave trade became one of the most profitable operations for any European or American merchant captain. Kidnapped and sold by professional slavers, or taken prisoner by an enemy tribe, African captives were warehoused in seaside "factories," then sold to ship captains in exchange for manufactured goods, such as clothing and weapons, brought from Europe or Great Britain. Slaves

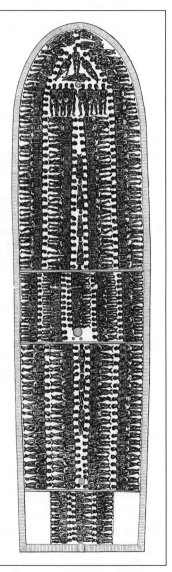

Slaves were chained belowdecks for the long voyage across the Atlantic Ocean.

were held belowdecks in chains for the long, often rough voyage across the Atlantic Ocean, during which 10 to 20 percent of them, on average, died of the heat, of disease, or of hunger and thirst. On arrival, slave traders either brought their cargo to market for a public auction or allowed buyers to board their ships and take immediate possession of their property. The slaves were sold or bartered for goods in demand in the Northern colonies or back in England. The majority of Africans who fell victim to this three-way, or triangular, trade wound up in the Caribbean or in South America, where the cultivation and processing of sugar had become the New World's most labor-intensive industry. The remainder were brought to North America, where planters were consolidating large plantations for the raising of cotton, rice, sugar, and tobacco.

The control of the slave trade by the English, and the ready supply of captives in West Africa, allowed the price of African slaves to drop sharply in the colonies during the eighteenth century. Despite the many deaths among slaves during the so-called Middle Passage from Africa to America, their trade was very profitable and the market for their labor secure among the burgeoning population of landholding British colonists. By this time, owning African slaves also presented advantages over the use of indentured servants. Their skin color, religion, language, and customs marked them as less than human to most whites; as a result, Africans were considered fit only for slavery and remained in bondage throughout their lives. The sons and daughters of slaves also became slaves, acquired at little cost to the owner, and strict laws regarding manumission (the granting of freedom) kept the percentage of Africans and African Americans in slavery high, especially in the tobacco-growing colonies of the Chesapeake region and in the rice and cotton country farther south.

Slaves and the Revolution

As much as the rules and punishment of the master, the laws of each colony controlled the lives of North American slaves. By colonial law, customarily, slaves could not vote, own property, or testify in court. They could not marry without the permission of their masters, and they could not travel freely. Owners had the right to beat, whip, brand, or imprison them for petty offenses or for attempted escape. Slave owners vied with each other in creating imaginative punishments, as historian Kenneth M. Stampp relates:

> A Maryland tobacco grower forced a hand [slave] to eat the worms he failed to pick off the tobacco leaves. A Mississippian gave a runaway a wretched time by requiring him to sit at the table and eat his evening meal with the white family. A Louisiana planter humiliated disobedient male field-hands by giving them "women's work" such as washing clothes, by dressing them in women's clothing, and by exhibiting them on a scaffold wearing a red flannel cap.[1]

Slave owners also had the right to break up slave families any time they wished. (In most colonies, there were also certain rules against killing slaves; such an act usually brought a fine.) Many owners punished slaves who taught themselves to read or write, or who practiced any form of religion, either African or Christian.

With the legal and economic system upholding their bondage, black slaves developed into an essential ingredient of the Southern plantation economy, which depended largely on markets in the Northern colonies or in Europe. Slaves made up a majority of the population of colonial South Carolina, and the colony of Georgia, originally having banned slavery entirely, overturned this ban in 1750 so that its white farmers could compete with their neighbors in the Carolinas. Slave-grown tobacco made the Chesapeake region one of the wealthiest in colonial America. Although some farms in the North had large companies of slaves, in general, slavery held much less importance in the Northern colonies, where most Africans worked as extra hands in small manufacturing businesses, as household servants, or on smaller farms in the countryside.

In the 1760s and 1770s, the movement for liberty from

English rule forced many colonial leaders to question the institution of slavery. Although some concluded that Africans by their nature must and would always remain slaves, others suggested that a revolution founded in "life, liberty, and the pursuit of happiness" should extend these natural rights to everyone, regardless of their nation of origin or their legal status as property. Nevertheless, the founders of the United States, ingenious in establishing a system of representative republican government, could not solve the problem of when and how to grant freedom to the slaves. They also wrestled with the question of how slavery would affect the representation of each state in the national legislature

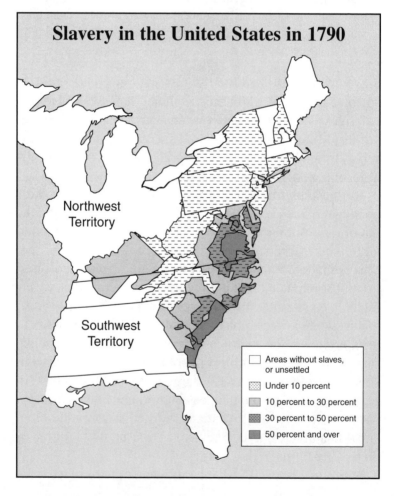

Slavery in the United States in 1790

Northwest Territory

Southwest Territory

☐ Areas without slaves, or unsettled

▦ Under 10 percent

▨ 10 percent to 30 percent

▦ 30 percent to 50 percent

■ 50 percent and over

(Southern states with large slave populations would not grant citizenship to blacks, of course, but they wanted their fair share of representatives in Congress). In *Miracle at Philadelphia,* Catherine Drinker Bowen relates that the delegates had different priorities:

> No delegate had come to Philadelphia hoping for anything so drastic as to outlaw slavery from the United States, even those who hated it most. This was not a legislative body, to make laws. It was the business of delegates to create a Constitution for the country as it existed, and if slavery made a mockery of the words freedom, liberty, the rights of man, then those who thought so could have their say on the floor. Without disrupting the Convention and destroying the Union they could do no more.[2]

The issue would be resolved by compromise. By the U.S. Constitution, ratified by 1787, each slave would be worth three-fifths of a free individual in determining how many representatives each state would send to the House of Representatives. In addition, the slave trade would be legally ended—after a period of twenty years.

The South, the North, and Abolition

It was a Yankee inventor named Eli Whitney who gave the strongest impetus to Southern slavery after the American Revolution. Six years after the Constitution was ratified, Whitney created the cotton gin, a device that separated seeds from fiber in the short-staple cotton grown in inland areas of the South. Before Whitney's invention, cotton seeds had to be separated from cotton fiber by hand, a time-consuming task that had limited cotton cultivation in North America. After Whitney's invention, large and small cotton plantations became practical, even with the expense of slave labor. Within eight years of the first cotton gin, the South increased its annual export of cotton from 150,000 tons to 17 million tons. As the Deep South states of Alabama, Mississippi, Louisiana, and Texas entered the Union, cotton became the South's most important crop and the country's most important export. In a short time, it also made the states of the Deep South economically dependent on what came to be known as "the peculiar institution"—slave labor.

Meanwhile, the importation of slaves had been banned by federal law in 1808. This law ended the arrival of slave ships in North America, but it did not end the buying and selling of slaves in important markets such as Richmond, Virginia; Charleston, South Carolina; and New Orleans, Louisiana. As cotton production expanded in the Deep South, many planters in tobacco states such as Virginia and Maryland, suffering from a stagnant tobacco market, sold their slaves to the planters of the Deep South. Thousands of African American families were broken up and sold down the Mississippi River to work in the region's cotton fields. Slaves made up a growing proportion of the population in the Deep South, more than half in the states of Mississippi and South Carolina. At the same time, the slave population was growing on its own, thanks to better diet and working conditions in North America as compared to the Caribbean and South America. No longer in need of imports from Africa, the Southern slave system became self-supporting, and by 1825, about one-third of all slaves in the New World lived in the southern United States.

A much different situation was coming to pass in the North. Since the American Revolution, several northern states had passed laws emancipating slaves, which encouraged a growing movement for the abolition of slavery. The abolition movement was pioneered by the Quakers of Pennsylvania, who first protested slavery in the late seventeenth century. In 1777 Vermont became the first state to abolish slavery. One by one, the other Northern states followed, as did the slave colonies elsewhere in the hemisphere. In 1834 the British Parliament abolished slavery in the Caribbean, and several South American countries had already banned slavery within their borders.

The people of the South saw their economic interests, and their way of life, threatened by abolitionism. A growing antagonism over the issue began to divide the largely rural South from the increasingly industrial North. The room for compromise grew small, then disappeared. According to historian Stanley M. Elkins,

To the Northern reformer, every other concrete fact concerning slavery was dwarfed by its character as a moral evil—as an obscenity condemned by God and universally offensive to humanity. The Southerner replied in kind; slavery was a positive moral good—a necessary arrangement sanctioned in Scripture and thus by God Himself, in which an inferior race must live under the domination of a superior.[3]

While abolitionists supported their cause with the argument for liberty given in the Declaration of Independence, Southerners pointed to the Tenth Amendment of the Constitution, in which powers not specifically granted to the federal government are reserved for the states. In other words, the states had rights, including the right to regulate and enforce the laws concerning slavery, that could not be abrogated by the federal government.

Slave Culture

In the meantime, among the abolitionists a back-to-Africa movement emerged in the early 1800s. Its advocates accepted the idea advanced by slavery's supporters: that freed slaves would never be able to adapt to white society, and that emancipation would unleash destructive social forces that would tear the country apart. But most of these "reverse colonialists" eventually gave up their idea as unworkable. Not only would returning slaves to Africa be too expensive, and disruptive to the national economy, the slaves themselves had established a culture of their own that was completely foreign to the African continent.

In some regions, such as the string of narrow and low-lying islands off the coast of South Carolina, African culture survived virtually intact, benefiting from slaves' isolation and from the fact that owners were largely absent. But among the majority of slaves, original African culture was gradually, over several generations, replaced by a new culture with its own religion, music, language, and habits of dress and daily life. This new African American culture combined African tradition with the European-descended traditions and religion of slave owners. The people of New

Orleans witnessed African-derived dance and music, medicine, and dress. African styles were adapted by American blacks in the arts of woodcarving and quilting. African vocabulary and syntax were transformed by slave speech into an entirely new dialect of English.

In the early nineteenth century, during the religious revival known as the Second Great Awakening, many African Americans also adopted Protestant Christian rites. White missionaries traveled between the Southern plantations, bringing the gospel to a people set apart as heathens by earlier white generations. But as Southern slave owners realized, the missions often accomplished much more than religious conversion. According to historian Edgar J. McManus, "[Slaves] saw . . . that black Christians were excluded from voting on church matters, barred from church offices, and segregated from the rest of the congregation at religious meetings. Instead of inculcating respect for religion, proselytization more often nurtured contempt for white hypocrisy."[4]

Where slaves were banned from practicing religion of any sort, they met in secret in hidden groves and clearings to worship and pray on their own. By the time of the Civil War the slaves of the South had created a widespread, independent black church that would survive both the war and Reconstruction (the period of change and adjustment that would come in the war's aftermath).

The Southern Reaction

In the early 1800s abolition and back-to-Africa movements spread through the cities of the North, encouraged by antislavery books, articles, speeches, and sermons. Nevertheless, a large proportion of white Americans, even Northern white Americans, still viewed slavery as an unfortunate evil that could never be properly solved. To recolonize the slaves to Africa was impractical; to abolish slavery entirely would bring a flood of jobless blacks into the cities, causing social and economic chaos. During the 1830s William Lloyd Garrison, a Northern journalist, founded the *Liberator* to fight for an end to slavery, but he found himself nearly lynched in the liberal city of Boston—the revolutionary "Cradle of Liberty"—for his stand.

The abolition movement also brought a strong counter-reaction in the South where—as Southern planters were always quick to point out—cotton was providing the nation with its most lucrative export. Although Southerners had been at the forefront of the move for democratic government and liberty in the eighteenth century, nineteenth-century slaveholders still dependent on cotton clung to the traditions of the past and their rural, agricultural way of life.

The Southern planters also resisted industrialization for its need of a skilled and educated class of laborers, which they knew would come in large part from among freed slaves. In Southern literature, the well-ordered plantation represented social harmony whereas the city represented an evil that had brought crime and violence, along with dangerously violent revolutionary movements, to Europe. Slavery's proponents claimed that slaves were better off as slaves than they ever would be as free citizens let loose in the cold and uncaring world of the factory, where greedy capitalists showed a peculiar cruelty of their own by providing neither food nor shelter to their poorly paid workers.

Southern newspapers, journals, and books railed against the North, sometimes out of conviction and sometimes from a desire for best-selling controversy. Southern writers derided Northern abolitionists as meddling busybodies and Northern abolitionist legislators as interfering, would-be tyrants. The states had rights, they insisted, and through legislation several Southern states freely asserted those rights by abolishing the manumission (freeing) of slaves. South Carolina passed this law in 1820, Mississippi in 1822, Arkansas in 1858, and Maryland and Alabama in 1860.

Not coincidentally, the economy of the South began lagging that of the North. The cities of the South remained relatively small and their industries undeveloped. The percentage of the nation's population living in the South declined as immigrants arrived in Northern ports and as new states were settled in the West and Northwest. The South depended on Northern banks for credit and on Northern transportation companies to bring their goods to foreign markets. Many observers traveling through the South remarked on the region's poverty and backwardness as compared to the well-ordered fields and prosperous towns of the North. In their writings, most of these observers came to the same conclusion: The institution of slavery, by inspiring repression and closed-minded political and economic thinking, was dooming the South to a permanent second-class status within the United States.

Through the mid-1800s, slave owners constituted a shrinking proportion of the white population of the South (even as the slave population continued to increase, reaching 3.8 million by 1860). The economic gap between slaveholders and nonslaveholders grew wider as whites unable to buy and maintain slaves saw slave owners consolidating larger estates. Economic power also translated into political power: Slave owners made up a majority in Southern state legislatures and in the Southern courts. Most Southern governors were slaveholders; most Southern senators and representatives in Washington were slaveholders. The voices raised against slavery in the South remained in a weak minority, and individuals opposing slavery found their initiatives quashed under the economic and political power of the slave-owning aristocracy. The last organized legislative movement in the South against slavery took place in the Virginia state house in the 1830s (in the wake of Nat Turner's bloody slave rebellion). The move to restrict slavery in Virginia, however, was easily defeated by the better-organized slave owners and their representatives.

The controversy over slavery grew more strident as the decades passed. Abolitionists ventured south to escort runaways into the free cities of Philadelphia and New York. Slave runaways drifted over dangerous back roads to disappear into the mixed populations of towns such as New Orleans and Charleston. While Northern legislators pressed to ban slavery in the new western territories, a system of safe houses known as the Underground Railroad was set up to help slave fugitives escape to the North and to Canada.

The Fugitive Slave Law

In reaction to these threats and to the problem of runaways and the Underground Railroad, a federal Fugitive Slave Law was passed at the initiative of Southern legislators in 1850. The law set a prison term of six months and a two thousand dollar fine for anyone found to be helping a runaway. In addition, the new law authorized federal officials to extradite runaways to their place of origin, no matter how long they had been absent, merely on the word of their owners and without trial.

The Fugitive Slave Law brought a storm of outrage in the North. Abolitionists held meetings and indignant newspaper editors bemoaned the takeover of Congress by Southern interests. In the North, public opinion gradually turned against slavery, often as a matter of regional pride against the combative, presumptuous Southerners, and the battle lines between the North and the South began to form. The law prompted renewed efforts to aid runaways to Canada and also inspired Harriet Beecher Stowe to write *Uncle Tom's Cabin*, the novel that brought the slavery question and abolitionism to the masses. In 1854, in Boston—the same city that had nearly lynched William Lloyd Garrison a generation earlier—citizens rioted over the transportation of the fugitive slave Anthony Burns, who had to be escorted by federal troops—at great cost to the taxpayers—aboard the vessel returning him to Virginia.

At the same time, Northern states were passing their own set of laws relating to fugitives. The first of these personal liberty laws was passed in Indiana in 1824. They prohibited state officials from capturing or holding runaway slaves and required that slave owners demanding the return of their fugitive property submit to a jury trial. Thirteen Northern states had personal liberty laws on the books by 1860, justifying their actions by the doctrine of "nullification"—the belief that states could override or ignore inconvenient fed-

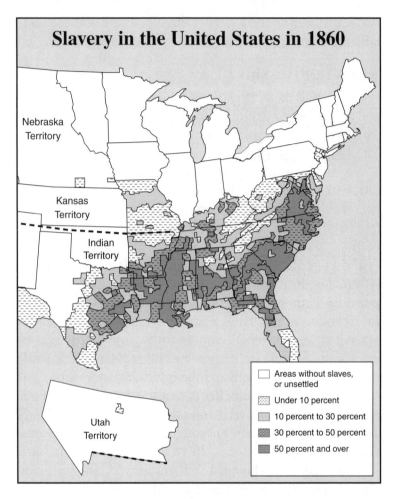

Slavery in the United States in 1860

Nebraska Territory

Kansas Territory

Indian Territory

Utah Territory

☐ Areas without slaves, or unsettled

▨ Under 10 percent

▨ 10 percent to 30 percent

▨ 30 percent to 50 percent

■ 50 percent and over

eral laws. Ironically, the leading proponents of nullification were Southerners, intent on ignoring lawmakers in Washington when it suited their interests. In its early years, nullification had been applied by the Virginians James Madison and Thomas Jefferson to the federal Alien and Sedition Acts. Later, South Carolina employed nullification to overturn a hated federal tariff.

Secession and War

In the 1850s the debate over slavery spread into all areas of the nation's political business. The legislative struggle had begun with the Missouri Compromise of 1820, which banned slavery in new territories lying north of Missouri's southern boundary. From that point on, a bitter conflict arose whenever settlement or war added new territory to the United States. As historian David M. Potter explains,

> The history of the slavery contest was a record of paroxysms arising from territorial rivalry, and of lulls following upon territorial compromise. . . . This cycle always began with the acquisition or opening of a new territory. Such an event proved the signal for a conflict between slavery expansionists and exclusionists. As the violence of their contest increased so far as to threaten the security of the country, moderates and Unionists became alarmed and intervened to impose some sort of territorial adjustment, whereupon the excitement diminished and the country lapsed into a period of relative quiet.[5]

The question of the extension of slavery to the West again came up with the settlement of Kansas and Nebraska. By the Kansas-Nebraska Act of 1854, these new territories would subject the legality of slavery to a popular vote. The compromise did not bring peace to the West. Instead, it brought all-out war between slavery's supporters and opponents on the frontier. During this conflict, a fierce Northern abolitionist named John Brown fought and murdered pro-slavery opponents in a bloody premonition of a national civil war.

The Kansas-Nebraska Act prompted disgruntled politicians to form the Republican Party in 1854. The party's fundamental cause was "free soil," or prevention of slavery in new states. In 1856 the Republicans put forth John Fremont as their presidential candidate. Fremont lost that year to Democrat James Buchanan, but the election of 1860 was a different story. Republican Abraham Lincoln, who carried the free-soil banner, was voted into office on his promise to keep new territories free and allow slave states to keep their slaves. Many observers sensed the clouds of war forming over the United States, and the presentiments had grown stronger with John Brown's raid on the federal arsenal at Harpers Ferry, Virginia, in 1859. Seeking to incite a national slave revolt, Brown became a martyr to abolitionists and a villain to slave owners. He was captured and executed by the state of Virginia after staging what many consider to be the first battle of the Civil War.

Southern leaders believed that the election of Lincoln spelled doom for the institution of slavery. Instead of allowing the Northern Republicans to dictate to their state legislatures and see new antislavery laws put into effect, these leaders made the fateful decision to withdraw from the Union entirely. Secession began with South Carolina in December 1860 and was followed by six more states early the next year. At a convention of secessionist states at Montgomery, Alabama, the Confederate States of America was founded, with Jefferson Davis as the first president. In April 1861 Confederate guns opened fire on Fort Sumter, located in the harbor at Charleston, South Carolina, and the Civil War began.

Lincoln and many other Northerners loudly proclaimed, in the first months of the war, that slavery was but a secondary issue in the conflict, and that the proper goal of the fight was the restoration of the Union. But as the war dragged on, and as public support waned and the supply of volunteers dried up, Lincoln realized that a new and different justification was needed. On January 1, 1863, Lincoln delivered the Emancipation Proclamation, freeing all of the slaves within those states that had seceded. Although the proclamation could not be enforced in rebel territory and it didn't apply to slaveholding states that had stayed within the Union, it imparted a much-needed fighting spirit to the North. African Americans joined the ranks of the Union army, bringing credit to the antislavery position that blacks would readily fight for their freedom. Seen as fighting against slavery, the Union also drew the support of European nations that had been leaning toward supporting the South.

The Legacy of Slavery

The Civil War ended in April 1865, with the battered and starving armies of the South laying down their arms in Virginia and North Carolina. Slavery came to a constitutional end with the passage and ratification of the Thirteenth and Fourteenth Amendments in 1865. The Thirteenth Amendment banned slavery throughout the United States; the Fourteenth Amendment granted full citizenship to all persons, black or white, born within the United States and extended voting rights to all former male slaves. The amendment also turned the "three-fifths" African American into a whole person for the purposes of congressional representation, and set down the doctrines of "due process" and "equal protection," by which all citizens of the United States may assert their civil rights when subjected to arrest and trial.

The legacy of slavery in the South comprised many decades of conflict between former slaves and white Southerners determined to keep some vestiges of the South's identity and its traditional social order. Although slavery had been banned and discredited, discrimination against African Americans remained, as did the South's economic backwardness, worsened by the damages of the war. Slavery ultimately inspired the formation of criminal militias such as the Ku Klux Klan, which was established by former Confederate officers and was later revived in the 1920s, as well as segregation in churches and schools that continued through the 1960s. Slavery left the country with mutual suspicion and distrust between blacks and whites, and between the North and the South, and difficult legal, social, and political problems that have continued into the twenty-first century.

Notes

1. Kenneth M. Stampp, *The Peculiar Institution: Slavery in the Ante-Bellum South.* New York: Alfred A. Knopf, 1982, p. 172.

2. Catherine Drinker Bowen, *Miracle at Philadelphia: The Story of the Constitutional Convention, May to September 1787.* Boston: Little, Brown, 1966, p. 200.

3. Stanley M. Elkins, *Slavery: A Problem in American Institutional and Intellectual Life.* Chicago: University of Chicago Press, 1968, p. 36.

4. Edgar J. McManus, *Black Bondage in the North.* Syracuse, NY: Syracuse University Press, 1973, p. 206.

5. David M. Potter, *Lincoln and His Party in the Secession Crisis.* New Haven, CT: Yale University Press, 1942, pp. 65–66.

Chapter 1

The Slave Trade

Chapter Preface

The nations of Europe began planting colonies in the Western Hemisphere in the late fifteenth century. Slavery soon followed the first European explorers and settlers to the New World. Slaves provided a solution to a critical labor shortage in these colonies, which produced valuable cash crops and raw materials. The earliest New World slavery was geared toward large-scale commercial planting on estates in the Caribbean region and later on the North American mainland. The owners of these estates needed as many hands as possible for the production of sugar, tobacco, rice, indigo, and, later, cotton. For a dependable source of labor, they had only one place to turn: the African slave trade.

This market was served by slave merchants operating out of ports in Europe, especially England, and in North America. The slavers left their home ports with holds full of manufactured goods to be traded for captives held along the western coast of Africa. Native Africans took part as middlemen in the slave trade, bartering their own captives to the whites for the goods unavailable on their own continent.

Europeans made slavery into an important commercial activity in its own right, but they were not the first to deal in African slaves. Africans had been trading slaves with Arabs and the cities of North Africa for centuries along well-established caravan routes that led through the Sahara Desert. Some slaves were caught in battle; others were kidnapped. Some were sentenced to slavery for a crime. All slaves sold to Europeans had one thing in common: an experience of the transatlantic voyage known as the Middle Passage, a journey of anguish, violence, and hunger that brought death to hundreds of thousands of African captives.

In all, about 10 million slaves were brought across the Atlantic until the slave trade ended in the nineteenth century.

About six hundred thousand slaves arrived in the United States by the time the importation of slaves was outlawed in 1808. After this date, the domestic slave trade continued as briskly as ever within those states that still permitted slavery, even as the debate between pro-slavery and abolitionist factions grew bitter.

A Voyage to West Africa

Joseph Hawkins

New Yorker Joseph Hawkins had voyaged to Charleston in search of his fortune in the wealthy port city. In 1793, soon after his arrival, he found a berth aboard the slaving ship *Charleston*, bound for Guinea (West Africa). Although by this time it was illegal to import slaves into Charleston, the city's sea merchants were still buying and capturing slaves in Africa and selling them in the West Indies.

After reaching the African coast, the ship's captain asks Hawkins to lead an expedition into the interior, where recent fighting between the Ebo and Galla tribes has brought an opportunity for buying some prisoners of war. The slave trade does not come easily or naturally to Hawkins, who is affected by the agony and despair of the African prisoners. But the author consoles himself with the thoughts that he needs the work, that he can do nothing to stop the traffic in humans, and that African slaves might even find life easier once they reach the plantation and its dependable food and shelter.

Hawkins barters with the victorious Ebo leaders, then ferries his prisoners downriver to the coast. Not all goes smoothly, however, as the prisoners take advantage of the inattention of their guards to revolt, and Hawkins—lacking a gun or a sword—has to use his wits to end the fighting and save his own life.

From Joseph Hawkins, *A History of a Voyage to the Coast of Africa, and Travels into the Interior of That Country; Containing Particular Descriptions of the Climate and Inhabitants, and Interesting Particulars Concerning the Slave Trade* (Philadelphia: S.C. Ustick, 1797).

We sailed from Charleston the 1st of December 1793, on board the ship *Charleston*, J. Connelly master, burthen 400 Tons; and after a passage partly boisterous, and frequently becalmed for several days, we made the isles of Delos on the 17th January 1794.

These islands are nine in number, and afford harbours and safe anchorage in deep water for ships of any burthen; they are six leagues [about 18 miles] from the main land of Africa, in 12 deg. 30 min. south latitude. They are inhabited by French and English factors, who find their account in living on those islands in preference to the main [land], particularly from the circumstances of accommodation for their ships, which lie here with the greatest safety in all weathers, and that their slaves cannot easily escape. The slaves are in those islands suffered to go at large, without chains, contrary to the customs on the continent. The surface of the islands is barren and rocky, but there is abundance of fine fresh water; and provisions are procured with facility.

War and Opportunity

From the factors [slave-trading agents] here we learned that the Ebo and Galla Kings had been at war, the latter of whom having been defeated, and a great part of his army had fallen into the hands of the conqueror, they therefore advised us to proceed for the Reyo-pongo river, about 25 leagues [about 75 miles] south westward, and from thence the access to the Ebo nation would be easily secured, by a passage up that river and from thence by land, about three hundred miles from the mouth of this river; they furnished us with further directions, and assured us of a certain and good trade.

Agreeably to this information, we provided ourselves with such necessaries as the factors could afford us, and proceeded for the Reyo-pongo, which we made on the 5th of February, and after choosing a proper situation, came to anchor in a handsome harbour within the northern bank. . . .

On the 6th February we were visited by numbers of the natives, who offered to barter with us fruit and ivory for our hardwares; but finding after we had exchanged a few articles, that they belonged to a nation which had been be-fore represented to us as thinly inhabited, and that we could not accommodate ourselves here as we wished, we made use of them to obtain information concerning the country of the Ebo king. We fortunately found an inter-preter acquainted with that country and the trade, him we engaged, and an expedition was immediately determined upon by the captain. . . .

He proposed that I should go and see the prisoners; we accordingly crossed to the southeastern side of the rivulet, where at the lower side of the town, we found them confined in a large area within a thick stockade, on the outside of which was a trench: the inside was divided into parcels, and huts irregularly constructed, and the entrance as well as the whole circuit, was guarded by men with spears.

A Peculiar Horror

We commonly find ourselves impressed with emotions of horror or compassion, on entering places where our fellow men are doomed to punishment or thraldom [slavery]. In the scene before me, the ear was not indeed dinned with the clanking of heavy fetters, but was horrible in its peculiar way. The captives were destitute for the most part of even their necessary covering, and bound indiscriminately to-gether by the hands and legs, the cords being again fastened to the ground by stakes; they were loosed a few at a time once every day, when each was permitted to eat the only meal they were allowed, consisting of rice and palm oil. Benevolence, however, sometimes broke through the rigours of a savage life, and occasionally alleviated the sufferings of the weakly, or the wounded with milk or other neces-saries: their condition was on the whole deplorable.

I had often in the course of the voyage, and of the jour-ney, rebuked myself for having embarked in the African trade, but found a consolation in the reflection, that it was not from a malicious inclination or avaricious disposition, that I had embarked in it, but from the pressing call of ne-cessity, and at a time when my dissent could not alter or obstruct the undertaking. On the present occasion, however, I was fully convinced the removal of these poor wretches even into the slavery of the West-Indies, would be an act of humanity, rather than one exposed to censure.

We passed through the whole range of the place of confinement, the old chief pointing out to me those who were the greatest warriors of the Galla nation. He then intimated to me that I might choose such of them as I should think proper and agree on what he was to receive in return. I agreed to do so, but requested that I might have an opportunity of conversing with them, and choosing such as would go with me voluntarily, if any could be found. To this he readily assented; and for the next week I continued to visit them daily, and took occasion through my interpreter, to exhibit as flattering a prospect to their future situation in America, should they go with me, as I thought was just in itself, and favorable to their wishes. . . .

Having arranged matters on this subject to my mind, I mentioned to the old king the several articles which I proposed exchanging with him, and showing specimens of such few articles as I had brought, proposed dispatching a person to the ship with a letter, directing the Captain to send a shallop [small boat] with goods to the mouth of the little Congo, and that rafts should be ready with hands to convey them up the rest of the way. The Galla nation having suffered so much by their last war, had now became fearful of molesting or interfering with the Ebo people, a circumstance, which if we had previously known, would have saved us a long circuitous and troublesome journey, which might now be performed with ease in one half the time. . . .

Trading Goods

On the 3d of April, while I was on an excursion abroad, one of the messengers returned from the ship, and I found him before me at my hut in the evening, with a packet from the Captain, advising me of the goods which he had sent by the shallop, to the mouth of the little Congo, and giving me directions how to proceed.

The information being communicated to the old chief, he informed me he would send a number of experienced old men with me, to choose such articles as they should approve and after three days, provisions and horses being provided, we set out, the company consisting of six of the deputation, with some of their families, a number of persons to carry provisions and goods, and my two wives. We had nearly 100 miles to go, which engaged us six days; riding proved very unpleasant to me, on account of the heat and the want of a saddle. We found the boats as we were directed, and a cargo of brandy, rum, gin, and tobacco, a few coarse guns, some ammunition, swords, knives, spears, and ornament, such as rings of various kinds, for the legs, arms, and fingers, some gilt and plated breast plates for their warriors, tinsel laces [ornamental braids], and some glass-ware. An assortment so extensive and rich in their eyes, had never been there before; and bargains were very soon made for goods, in exchange for 100 slaves, (being ordered not to bring down more) for the rest I procured ivory and gold, in dust and bars. In these dealings I found my wives of more use to me than my companion Hurdee, for they sincerely studied my interest, while he studied to profit himself. . . .

The slaves that I had purchased were young men, many of whom being eager to escape from their bondage in Ebo, preferred the evil they "knew not of" to that which they then felt; but the majority were evidently affected with grief at their approaching departure.

Arrangements were made and a sufficient body of the Ebo people undertook to accompany me as a guard to the place of embarkation; provisions were provided for the journey, so that each of the slaves was well fed, and a load of provisions or goods given him to carry. They were tied to poles in rows, four feet apart; a loose wicker bandage round the neck of each, connected him to the pole, and the arms being pinioned by a bandage affixed behind above the elbows, they had sufficient room to feed, but not to loose themselves, or commit any violence; and as the guard was provided with arms, we had nothing to apprehend during the night, as we divided the Ebo people into parties, one of which slept while the other watched. . . .

Comforting Assurances

This journey was extremely different in its nature from that in which I had last passed this way; the giddy pranks of the vain, or the inebriated Ebo, was woefully contrasted by the sullen melancholy, and deep sighs of the poor Galla prisoners; often did they look back with eyes flowing with tears, turn sudden round and gaze, seeming to part with reluctance, even from their former bondage. It was excessively

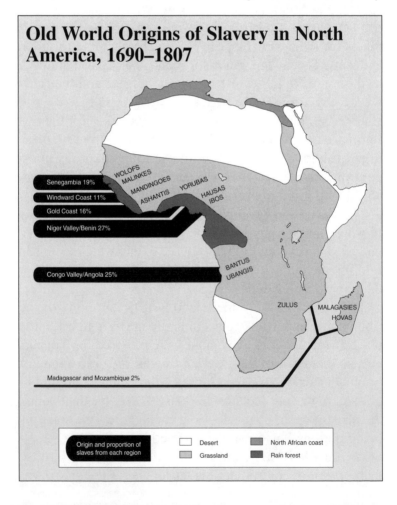

Old World Origins of Slavery in North America, 1690–1807

Senegambia 19%
Windward Coast 11%
Gold Coast 16%
Niger Valley/Benin 27%
Congo Valley/Angola 25%
Madagascar and Mozambique 2%

WOLOFS
MALINKES
MANDINGOES
ASHANTIS
YORUBAS
HAUSAS
IBOS
BANTUS
UBANGIS
ZULUS
MALAGASIES
HOVAS

Origin and proportion of slaves from each region
Desert
Grassland
North African coast
Rain forest

affecting to me, but I considered that death might have been their fate otherwise, and I endeavoured to reconcile them to their condition, by representing flattering accounts of the country to which they were going; that the bonds they then bore were only to prevent their flight; that they should be at liberty where they were going, and have plenty to eat, drink, etc. These assurances occasioned a temporary composure, and we at length arrived at the place of our embarkation; two boats had been brought up, as the shallop drew too much water; the slaves were put on board, and necessarily in irons brought for the purpose. This measure occasioned one of the most affecting scenes I ever witnessed: their hopes with my assurances had buoyed them up on the road; but a change from the cordage to iron fetters, rent their hopes and hearts together: their wailings were torturing beyond what words can express; but delay at this crisis would have been fatal; the boat's crews were acquainted with the duty, and they were all safely embarked. . . .

We soon lost sight of them in a winding of the river; and continued going down with the current till night; the slaves seemed every hour to feel their situation more grievously, and I ordered them each a dram of liquor which for a while exhilarated their spirits, and quieted their cares. . . . We furnished the slaves with provisions, but whether through grief or sullenness, very few of them would partake of any refreshments beside water.

Trouble in the Boats

As soon as we had light we unmoored, and before noon we reached our shallop, extremely fatigued from the heat and closeness of the air, the banks of each side as we passed, being overgrown with wood and thicket, obstructing its free circulation. We had now another disagreeable piece of duty to execute, *viz.* the removal of the slaves from the small boats into the shallop; they were in want of room, and it was suggested to loose six of them at a time; we accordingly moved to the centre of the river, and being moored by a grapling [small anchor], began to remove them; they appeared generally more quiet, and willing to act as we directed by the interpreter than usual, and had now all been removed, and placed below, but the last six, whom we suffered to remain on deck; when we had got under way, and were passing through a narrow part of the river, two of them found means to jump overboard; a sailor who was in the small boat astern seized one of them by the arms, and the end of a rope being thrown to him, the slave was taken on board, though not without some difficulty. The others who had been at the oars, seeing their fellows, one of them seized, and the other struck on the head with a pole, set up a scream, which was echoed by the rest below; those that were loose made an effort to throw two of the sailors overboard; the rest, except the one in the boat and at the helm, being asleep: the noise had now aroused them, and the scream had impressed them with some degree of terror; they seized on the guns and bayonets that lay ready, and rushed upon the slaves, five of whom from below had got loose, and were endeavouring to set the rest free, while those we had to deal with above, were threatening to sacrifice us to their despair. These transactions were but the events of a moment; I had neither gun nor sword, and to retire in search of either, would have been to give the slaves a decisive superiority; I laid hold of the palloon [maneuvering] stick, and had raised it to strike one of them who had nearly wrested a gun from one of the sailors, but before I could give the blow, I received a stroke of an oar, which severed my little finger from my hand; I know not how it was that I felt nothing of the severe pain for the moment, a slight twitch on the hand was the only sensation I experienced; the blow was broken that I had intended, but I renewed the effort, and with effect, for I levelled the fellow, and the sailor recovered his gun, whom I could not prevent from running the poor negro through the body; the hatch was open, and he fell among his fellows, who had, crowded, tied, and ironed as they were, to assist as far as they were able, by holding our legs, encouraging their companions, and shouting whenever those above did any thing that appeared likely to overcome one or other of us. We at length overpowered them; one only having escaped and one being killed, the rest were immediately bound in double irons, and took care from thence till our arrival at the ship, not to suffer any of them to take the air without being made fast. Five of the sailors were considerably, but not dangerously hurt, and of the slaves, those who had been riotous above and below, nine were severely wounded.

Taking Stock

We reached the ship in five days from our first embarkation, where we were received with much satisfaction; the officers had all provided themselves with three or four wives each, and rebuked me for not bringing mine along, alledging that they would, according to the account given by their messmates, bring a good price when we arrived in America. I was sorry, however, to find that two of our best seamen had expired during my absence, from the excessive fatigue of the ships duty, and the heat of the climate.

While I was away, the Captain had opened a trade in another channel, he had obtained 100 slaves in the place where he lay, beside gold and ivory; and had contracted with some French and English factors up the river Reyo Naunus, for the remainder of his cargo, and for his sea stores. We accordingly weighed anchor and stood for that river, which lies about 40 leagues [120 miles] N. of the Reyo Pongo, or in 10 deg. 40 min. south, and on the 16th of May arrived off the Cape, which forms one side of the southern outlet of that river. . . .

The whole number of slaves that we had now on board, I found about 500, of whom above 50 were then lying in a dangerous state of illness; it was time for us to depart, being now in the 13th of June, 1795. We accordingly got in our anchors, and procured six of the natives boats, with six men in each, to tow us down night and day, when the tide served.

The Middle Passage

Olaudah Equiano

A native of what is now Nigeria, Olaudah Equiano was born about 1745. At the age of ten, he and his sister were captured by thieves in search of marketable property—able-bodied children. He then experienced what later writers called the "Middle Passage," the horrific journey across the Atlantic Ocean, in which African captives were chained belowdecks for weeks before reaching their destination in the slave markets of North America.

After being granted his freedom in 1766, Equiano traveled all over the world, from North America to the Mediterranean to the Arctic Ocean. He took part in planning the first expedition of freed slaves to resettle in Africa in 1787. He also spoke throughout the colonies and in Great Britain for an end to slavery. He set down his experiences in his autobiography, which was first published in 1789—one of the earliest works of an African writer published in North America. The book gained a wide audience in the United States just as the movement for the abolition of slavery was beginning in the northern states.

The first object which saluted my eyes when I arrived on the coast was the sea, and a slave ship which was then riding at anchor and waiting for its cargo. These filled me with astonishment, which was soon converted into terror when I was carried on board. I was immediately handled and tossed up to see if I were sound by some of the crew,

From *The Interesting Narrative of the Life of Olaudah Equiano, or Gustavus Vassa, the African, Written by Himself* (Boston: 1789).

and I was now persuaded that I had gotten into a world of bad spirits and that they were going to kill me. Their complexions too differing so much from ours, their long hair and the language they spoke (which was very different from any I had ever heard) united to confirm me in this belief. Indeed such were the horrors of my views and fears at the moment that, if ten thousand worlds had been my own, I would have freely parted with them all to have exchanged my condition with that of the meanest slave in my own country. When I looked round the ship too and saw a large furnace or copper boiling and a multitude of black people of every description chained together, every one of their countenances expressing dejection and sorrow, I no longer doubted of my fate; and quite overpowered with horror and anguish, I fell motionless on the deck and fainted. When I recovered a little I found some black people about me, who I believed were some of those who had brought me on board and had been receiving their pay; they talked to me in order to cheer me, but all in vain. I asked them if we were not to be eaten by those white men with horrible looks, red faces, and loose hair. They told me I was not, and one of the crew brought me a small portion of spirituous liquor in a wine glass, but being afraid of him I would not take it out of his hand. One of the blacks therefore took it from him and gave it to me, and I took a little down my palate, which instead of reviving me, as they thought it would, threw me into the greatest consternation at the strange feeling it produced, having never tasted such any liquor before. Soon after this the blacks who brought me on board went off, and left me abandoned to despair.

Horrors of Every Kind

I now saw myself deprived of all chance of returning to my native country or even the least glimpse of hope of gaining the shore, which I now considered as friendly; and I even wished for my former slavery in preference to my present situation, which was filled with horrors of every kind, still heightened by my ignorance of what I was to undergo. I was not long suffered to indulge my grief; I was soon put down under the decks, and there I received such a salutation in my nostrils as I had never experienced in my life: so that with the loathsomeness of the stench and crying together, I became so sick and low that I was not able to eat, nor had I the least desire to taste anything. I now wished for the last friend, death, to relieve me; but soon, to my grief, two of the white men offered me eatables, and on my refusing to eat, one of them held me fast by the hands and laid me across I think the windlass, and tied my feet while the other flogged me severely. I had never experienced anything of this kind before, and although, not being used to the water, I naturally feared that element the first time I saw it, yet nevertheless could I have got over the nettings I would have jumped over the side, but I could not; and besides, the crew used to watch us very closely who were not chained down to the decks, lest we should leap into the water: and I have seen some of these poor African prisoners most severely cut for attempting to do so, and hourly whipped for not eating. This indeed was often the case with myself. In a little time after, amongst the poor chained men I found some of my own nation, which in a small degree gave ease to my mind. I inquired of these what was to be done with us; they gave me to understand we were to be carried to these white people's country to work for them. I then was a little revived, and thought if it were no worse than working, my situation was not so desperate: but still I feared I should be put to death, the white people looked and acted, as I thought, in so savage a manner; for I had never seen among my people such instances of brutal cruelty, and this not only shewn towards us blacks but also to some of the whites themselves. One white man in particular I saw, when we were permitted to be on deck, flogged so unmercifully with a large rope near the foremast that he died in consequence of it; and they tossed him over the side as they would have done a brute. This made me fear these people the more, and I expected nothing less than to be treated in the same manner. I could not help expressing my fears and apprehensions to some of

my countrymen: I asked them if these people had no country but lived in this hollow place (the ship): they told me
they did not, but came from a distant one. 'Then,' said I,
'how comes it in all our country we never heard of them?'
They told me because they lived so very far off. I then asked
where were their women? had they any like themselves? I
was told they had: 'and why,' said I, 'do we not see them?'
They answered, because they were left behind. I asked how
the vessel could go? They told me they could not tell, but
that there were cloths put upon the masts by the help of the
ropes I saw, and then the vessel went on; and the white men
had some spell or magic they put in the water when they
liked in order to stop the vessel.

Life Belowdecks

I was exceedingly amazed at this account and really thought
they were spirits. I therefore wished much to be from
amongst them for I expected they would sacrifice me: but
my wishes were vain, for we were so quartered that it was
impossible for any of us to make our escape. While we
stayed on the coast I was mostly on deck, and one day, to
my great astonishment, I saw one of these vessels coming
in with the sails up. As soon as the whites saw it they gave
a great shout, at which we were amazed; and the more so as
the vessel appeared larger by approaching nearer. At last she
came to an anchor in my sight, and when the anchor was let
go I and my countrymen who saw it were lost in astonishment to observe the vessel stop, and were now convinced it
was done by magic. Soon after this the other ship got her
boats out, and they came on board of us, and the people of
both ships seemed very glad to see each other. Several of the
strangers also shook hands with us black people, and made
motions with their hands, signifying I suppose we were to
go to their country; but we did not understand them. At last,
when the ship we were in had got in all her cargo, they made
ready with many fearful noises, and we were all put under
deck so that we could not see how they managed the vessel.
But this disappointment was the last of my sorrow. The

stench of the hold while we were on the coast was so intol-
erably loathsome that it was dangerous to remain there for
any time, and some of us had been permitted to stay on the
deck for the fresh air; but now that the whole ship's cargo
were confined together it became absolutely pestilential.
The closeness of the place and the heat of the climate, added
to the number in the ship, which was so crowded that each
had scarcely room to turn himself, almost suffocated us.
This produced copious perspirations, so that the air soon became unfit for respiration from a variety of loathsome
smells, and brought on a sickness among the slaves, of
which many died, thus falling victims to the improvident
avarice, as I may call it, of their purchasers. This wretched
situation was again aggravated by the galling of the chains,
now become insupportable, and the filth of the necessary
tubs [toilets], into which the children often fell and were almost suffocated. The shrieks of the women and the groans
of the dying rendered the whole a scene of horror almost in-
conceivable. Happily perhaps for myself I was soon reduced
so low here that it was thought necessary to keep me almost
always on deck, and from my extreme youth I was not put
in fetters. In this situation I expected every hour to share the
fate of my companions, some of whom were almost daily
brought upon deck at the point of death, which I began to
hope would soon put an end to my miseries. Often did I
think many of the inhabitants of the deep much more happy than myself. I envied them the freedom they enjoyed, and
as often wished I could change my condition for theirs.
Every circumstance I met with served only to render my
state more painful, and heighten my apprehensions and my
opinion of the cruelty of the whites.

A Want of Fresh Air

One day they had taken a number of fishes, and when they
had killed and satisfied themselves with as many as they
thought fit, to our astonishment who were on the deck,
rather than give any of them to us to eat as we expected,
they tossed the remaining fish into the sea again, although

we begged and prayed for some as well as we could, but in vain; and some of my countrymen, being pressed by hunger, took an opportunity when they thought no one saw them of trying to get a little privately; but they were discovered, and the attempt procured them some very severe floggings. One day, when we had a smooth sea and moderate wind, two of my wearied countrymen who were chained together (I was near them at the time), preferring death to such a life of misery, somehow made through the nettings and jumped into the sea: immediately another quite dejected fellow, who on account of his illness was suffered to be out of irons, also

Music on the Middle Passage

In his 1788 book The African Slave Trade, *Alexander Falconbridge gives a firsthand description of a transatlantic slave voyage. Falconbridge reveals that slave captains were paid for live slaves, not for dead ones, and for this reason they often force-fed their captives. Also mindful of the good physical condition of their Africans, which would bring a better profit, the slavers ordered their charges out on deck for short periods of exercise—in the form of dancing.*

Exercise being deemed necessary for the preservation of their health, they are sometimes obligated to dance, when the weather will permit their coming on deck. If they go about it reluctantly, or do not move with agility, they are flogged; a person standing by them all the time with a cat-o'-nine-tails in his hand for that purpose. Their music, upon these occasions, consists of a drum, sometimes with only one head; and when that is worn out, they do not scruple to make use of the bottom of one of the tubs. . . . The poor wretches are frequently compelled to sing also; but when they do so, their songs are generally, as may naturally be expected, melancholy lamentations of their exile from their native country.

followed their example; and I believe many more would very soon have done the same if they had not been prevented by the ship's crew, who were instantly alarmed. Those of us that were the most active were in a moment put down under the deck, and there was such a noise and confusion amongst the people of the ship as I never heard before, to stop her and get the boat out to go after the slaves. However two of the wretches were drowned, but they got the other and afterwards flogged him unmercifully for thus attempting to prefer death to slavery. In this manner we continued to undergo more hardships than I can now relate, hardships which are inseparable from this accursed trade. Many a time we were near suffocation from the want of fresh air, which we were often without for whole days together. This and the stench of the necessary tubs carried off many. During our passage I first saw flying fishes, which surprised me very much: they used frequently to fly across the ship and many of them fell on the deck. I also now first saw the use of the quadrant [telescope]; I had often with astonishment seen the mariners make observations with it, and I could not think what it meant. They at last took notice of my surprise, and one of them, willing to increase it as well as to gratify my curiosity, made me one day look through it. The clouds appeared to me to be land, which disappeared as they passed along. This heightened my wonder, and I was now more persuaded than ever that I was in another world and that everything about me was magic.

Arrival in Barbados

At last we came in sight of the island of Barbados, at which the whites on board gave a great shout and made many signs of joy to us. We did not know what to think of this, but as the vessel drew nearer we plainly saw the harbour and other ships of different kinds and sizes, and we soon anchored amongst them off Bridgetown. Many merchants and planters now came on board, though it was in the evening. They put us in separate parcels and examined us attentively. They also made us jump, and pointed to the land, signifying we were to go there. We thought by this we should be eaten by these ugly men, as they appeared to us; and when soon after we were all put down under the deck again, there was much dread and trembling among us, and nothing but bitter cries to be heard all the night from these apprehensions, insomuch that at last the white people got some old slaves from the land to pacify us. They told us we were not to be eaten but to work, and were soon to go on land where we should see many of our country people. This report eased us much; and sure enough soon after we were landed there came to us Africans of all languages. We were conducted immediately to the merchant's yard, where we were all pent up together like so many sheep in a fold without regard to sex or age. As every object was new to me everything I saw filled me with surprise. What struck me first was that the houses were built with storeys, and in every other respect different from those in Africa: but I was still more astonished on seeing people on horseback. I did not know what this could mean, and indeed I thought these people were full of nothing but magical arts. While I was in this astonishment one of my fellow prisoners spoke to a countryman of his about the horses, who said they were the same kind they had in their country. I understood them though they were from a distant part of Africa, and I thought it odd I had not seen any horses there; but afterwards when I came to converse with different Africans I found they had many horses amongst them, and much larger than those I then saw. We were not many days in the merchant's custody before we were sold after their usual manner, which is this: On a signal given, (as the beat of a drum) the buyers rush at once into the yard where the slaves are confined, and make choice of that parcel they like best. The noise and clamour with which this is attended and the eagerness visible in the countenances of the buyers serve not a little to increase the apprehensions of the terrified Africans, who may well be supposed to consider them as the ministers of that destruction to which they think themselves devoted. In this manner, without scruple, are relations and friends separated, most of them never to see each other again. I remember in the vessel in which I was brought over, in the men's apartment there were several brothers who, in the sale, were sold in different lots; and it was very moving on this occasion to see and hear their cries at parting. O, ye nominal Christians! might not an African ask you, Learned you this from your God who says unto you, Do unto all men as you would men should do unto you? Is it not enough that we are torn from our country and friends to toil for your luxury and lust of gain? Must every tender feeling be likewise sacrificed to your avarice? Are the dearest friends and relations, now rendered more dear by their separation from their kindred, still to be parted from each other and thus prevented from cheering the gloom of slavery with the small comfort of being together and mingling their sufferings and sorrows? Why are parents to lose their children, brothers their sisters, or husbands their wives? Surely this is a new refinement in cruelty which, while it has no advantage to atone for it, thus aggravates distress and adds fresh horrors even to the wretchedness of slavery.

A Day at the Slave Auctions

William Chambers

One of the nation's busiest slave markets, Richmond, Virginia, served as a way station for human goods being shipped from the east to the Deep South, where cotton growers operating large plantations kept up a high demand for slave labor. The slaves were sold and bought at small auction houses operated by independent businessmen, who opened their doors to traders as well as visitors.

In 1853, the Richmond slave market drew the attention of William Chambers, a publisher and philanthropist of Edinburgh, Scotland, who was visiting the United States. Fascinated by this curious business, Chambers strolls from one auction house to the next in the company of restless, bargain-hunting slaveowners. With attention to detail and the ironies of the situation, Chambers writes a detailed and dispassionate account of the slave trade as it was carried out in the United States.

S ituated on a high and sloping bank on the left side of the James River, Richmond is much less regular in outline than the greater number of American cities. Its streets, straggling in different directions on no uniform plan, are of an old-established appearance, with stores, churches, and numerous public buildings. Besides the principal thoroughfares, there are many narrow streets or lanes of a dismal, half-deserted appearance, generally dirty, and seemingly ill drained and ventilated. Everywhere, the number of black

From William Chambers, *Things as They Are in America* (Philadelphia: Lippincott, Grambo, 1854).

faces is considerable; for in a population of 27,000, as many as 9,000 are said to be slaves. The dwellings occupied by the lower classes of coloured people are of a miserable kind, resembling the worst brick-houses in the back-lanes of English manufacturing towns. In the upper part of the city, there are some rows of handsome villas, and in this quarter is a public square, with the Capitol, or seat of legislature, in a central and conspicuous situation. In walking through this public edifice towards dusk, I observed that it was guarded by an armed sentinel, the sight of whom had almost the startling effect of an apparition; for it was the first time I had seen a bayonet in the United States, and suggested the unpleasant reflection, that the large infusion of slaves in the composition of society was not unattended with danger.

The Business in Slaves

Although, in many respects, inferior in point of appearance as compared with the smart New-England cities, Richmond shewed various symptoms of prosperity and progress. A species of dock for shipping was in process of excavation adjoining the bridges, and several large cotton-factories were in the course of erection. In the streets in this lower quarter, there was an active trade in the packing and sale of tobacco, quantities of which, like faded weeds, were being carted to the factories by negroes. The cotton manufacture is carried on in several large establishments, and will soon be extended, but principally, I was told, by means of northern capital, and the employment of hired white labourers, who, for factory purposes, are said to be preferable to persons of colour.

Richmond is known as the principal market for the supply of slaves for the south—a circumstance understood to originate in the fact that Virginia, as a matter of husbandry, breeds negro labourers for the express purpose of sale. Having heard that such was the case, I was interested in knowing by what means and at what prices slaves are offered to purchasers. Without introductions of any kind, I was thrown on my own resources in acquiring this information. Fortunately, however, there was no impediment to encounter in the research. The exposure of ordinary goods in a store is not more open to the public than are the sales of slaves in Richmond. By consulting the local newspapers, I learned that the sales take place by auction every morning in the offices of certain brokers, who, as I understood by the terms of their advertisements, purchased or received slaves for sale on commission.

Where the street was in which the brokers conducted their business, I did not know; but the discovery was easily made. Rambling down the main street in the city, I found that the subject of my search was a narrow and short thoroughfare, turning off to the left, and terminating in a similar cross thoroughfare. Both streets, lined with brick-houses, were dull and silent. There was not a person to whom I could put a question. Looking about, I observed the office of a commission-agent, and into it I stepped. Conceive the idea of a large shop with two windows, and a door between; no shelving or counters inside; the interior a spacious, dismal apartment, not well swept; the only furniture a desk at one of the windows, and a bench at one side of the shop, three feet high, with two steps to it from the floor. I say, conceive the idea of this dismal-looking place, with nobody in it but three negro children, who, as I entered, were playing at auctioning each other. An intensely black little negro, of four or five years of age, was standing on the bench, or block, as it is called, with an equally black girl, about a year younger, by his side, whom he was pretending to sell by bids to another black child, who was rolling about the floor.

My appearance did not interrupt the merriment. The little auctioneer continued his mimic play, and appeared to enjoy the joke of selling the girl, who stood demurely by his side.

"Fifty dolla for de gal—fifty dolla—fifty dolla—I sell dis here fine gal for fifty dolla," was uttered with extraordinary volubility by the woolly-headed urchin, accompanied with appropriate gestures, in imitation, doubtless, of the scenes he had seen enacted daily on the spot. I spoke a few words to the little creatures, but was scarcely understood; and the fun went on as if I had not been present: so I left them, happy in rehearsing what was likely soon to be their own fate.

At another office of a similar character, on the opposite side of the street, I was more successful. Here, on inquiry, I was respectfully informed by a person in attendance, that the sale would take place the following morning at half-past nine o'clock.

At the Auction

Next day, I set out accordingly, after breakfast, for the scene of operations, in which there was now a little more life. Two or three persons were lounging about, smoking cigars; and, looking along the street, I observed that three red flags were projected from the doors of those offices in which sales were to occur. On each flag was pinned a piece of paper, notifying the articles to be sold. The number of lots was not great. On the first, was the following announcement:—"Will be sold this morning, at half-past nine o'clock, a Man and a Boy."

It was already the appointed hour; but as no company had assembled, I entered and took a seat by the fire. The office, provided with a few deal-forms and chairs, a desk at one of the windows, and a block accessible by a few steps, was tenantless, save by a gentleman who was arranging papers at the desk, and to whom I had addressed myself on the previous evening. Minute after minute passed, and still nobody entered. There was clearly no hurry in going to business. I felt almost like an intruder, and had formed the resolution of departing, in order to look into the other offices, when the person referred to left his desk, and came and seated himself opposite to me at the fire.

"You are an Englishman," said he, looking me steadily in the face; "do you want to purchase?"

"Yes," I replied, "I am an Englishman; but I do not intend to purchase. I am travelling about for information, and I shall feel obliged by your letting me know the prices at which negro servants are sold."

"I will do so with much pleasure," was the answer. "Do you mean fieldhands or house-servants?"

"All kinds," I replied; "I wish to get all the information I can."

With much politeness, the gentleman stepped to his desk, and began to draw up a note of prices. This, however, seemed to require careful consideration; and while the note was preparing, a lanky person, in a wide-awake [popular military-style] hat, and chewing tobacco, entered, and took the chair just vacated. He had scarcely seated himself, when, on looking towards the door, I observed the subjects of sale—the man and boy indicated by the paper on the red flag—enter together, and quietly walk to a form at the back of the shop, whence, as the day was chilly, they edged themselves towards the fire, in the corner where I was seated. I was now between the two parties—the white man on the right, and the old and young negro on the left—and I waited to see what would take place.

The sight of the negroes at once attracted the attention of Wide-awake. Chewing with vigour, he kept keenly eyeing the pair, as if to see what they were good for. Under this searching gaze, the man and boy were a little abashed, but said nothing. Their appearance had little of the repulsiveness we are apt to associate with the idea of slaves. They were dressed in a gray woollen coat, pants, and waistcoat, coloured cotton neckcloths, clean shirts, coarse woollen stockings, and stout shoes. The man wore a black hat; the boy was bareheaded. Moved by a sudden impulse, Wide-awake left his seat, and rounding the back of my chair, began to grasp at the man's arms, as if to feel their muscular capacity. He then examined his hands and fingers; and, last of all, told him to open his mouth and shew his teeth, which he did in a submissive manner. Having finished these examinations, Wide-awake resumed his seat, and chewed on in silence as before.

I thought it was but fair that I should now have my turn of investigation, and accordingly asked the elder negro what was his age. He said he did not know. I next inquired how old the boy was. He said he was seven years of age. On asking the man if the boy was his son, he said he was not—he was his cousin. I was going into other particulars, when the office-keeper approached, and handed me the note he had been preparing; at the same time making the observation that the market was dull at present, and that there never could be a more favourable opportunity of buying. I thanked him for the trouble which he had taken; and now submit a copy of his price-current:—

```
Best Men, 18 to 25 years old,  . . . . . . . . .1200 to 1300 dollars.
Fair    "        "       "    . . . . . . . . . . . . .  950 to 1050   "
Boys, 5 feet,  . . . . . . . . . . . . . . . . . . . . .  850 to  950   "
  "   4 feet 8 inches,  . . . . . . . . . . . . . .  700 to  800   "
  "   4 feet 5 inches,  . . . . . . . . . . . . . .  500 to  600   "
  "   4 feet,  . . . . . . . . . . . . . . . . . . . . .  375 to  450   "
Young Women,  . . . . . . . . . . . . . . . . . .  800 to 1000   "
Girls, 5 feet,  . . . . . . . . . . . . . . . . . . . . .  750 to  850   "
  "   4 feet 9 inches, . . . . . . . . . . . . . . .  700 to  750   "
  "   4 feet, . . . . . . . . . . . . . . . . . . . . . .  350 to  452   "
```
(Signed)

Richmond, Virginia

Perfect Humility

Leaving this document for future consideration, I pass on to a history of the day's proceedings. It was now ten minutes to ten o'clock, and Wide-awake and I being alike tired of waiting, we went off in quest of sales further up the street. Passing the second office, in which also nobody was to be seen, we were more fortunate at the third. Here, according to the announcement on the paper stuck to the flag, there were to be sold "A woman and three children; a young woman, three men, a middle-aged woman, and a little boy." Already a crowd had met, composed, I should think, of persons mostly from the cotton-plantations of the south. A few were seated near a fire on the right-hand side, and others stood round an iron stove in the middle of the apartment. The whole place had a dilapidated appearance. From a back-window, there was a view into a ruinous courtyard; beyond which, in a hollow, accessible by a side-lane, stood a shabby brick-house, on which the word *Jail* was inscribed in large black letters, on a white ground. I imagined it to be a depot for the reception of negroes.

On my arrival, and while making these preliminary observations, the lots for sale had not made their appearance. In about five minutes afterwards they were ushered in, one after the other, under the charge of a mulatto, who seemed to act as principal assistant. I saw no whips, chains, or any other engine of force. Nor did such appear to be required. All the lots took their seats on two long forms near the stove; none shewed any sign of resistance; nor did any one utter a word. Their manner was that of perfect humility and resignation.

As soon as all were seated, there was a general examination of their respective merits, by feeling their arms, look-

---

The Origins of American Slavery

Many of the founding fathers expressed deep regret that the colonists had allowed slavery to establish itself in the land they were trying to free from British domination. Indeed, some looked on slavery as one of the many grievances that they held against the British crown. George Mason of Virginia expressed this point, and made an eerily accurate prophecy, at the Constitutional Convention on August 22, 1787.

This infernal traffic originated in the avarice of British merchants. The British Government constantly checked the attempts of Virginia to put a stop to it. Slavery discourages arts and manufactures. The poor despise labor when performed by slaves. [Slaves] prevent the [immigration] of whites, who really enrich and strengthen a country. They produce the most pernicious effect on manners. Every master of slaves is born a petty tyrant. They bring the judgment of Heaven on a country. As nations cannot be rewarded or punished in the next world, they must be in this. By an inevitable chain of causes and effects, Providence punishes national sins by national calamities.

ing into their mouths, and investigating the quality of their hands and fingers—this last being evidently an important particular. Yet there was no abrupt rudeness in making these examinations—no coarse or domineering language was employed. The three negro men were dressed in the usual manner—in gray woollen clothing. The woman, with three children, excited my peculiar attention. She was neatly attired, with a coloured handkerchief bound round her head, and wore a white apron over her gown. Her children were all girls, one of them a baby at the breast, three months old, and the others two and three years of age respectively, rigged out with clean white pinafores. There was not a tear or an emotion visible in the whole party. Everything seemed to be considered as a matter of course; and the change of owners was possibly looked forward to with as much indifference as ordinary hired servants anticipate a removal from one employer to another.

While intending purchasers were proceeding with personal examinations of the several lots, I took the liberty of putting a few questions to the mother of the children. The following was our conversation:—

"Are you a married woman?"

"Yes, sir."

"How many children have you had?"

"Seven."

"Where is your husband?"

"In Madison County."

"When did you part from him?"

"On Wednesday—two days ago."

"Were you sorry to part from him?"

"Yes, sir," she replied with a deep sigh; "my heart was a'most broke."

"Why is your master selling you?"

"I don't know—he wants money to buy some land—suppose he sells me for that."

There might not be a word of truth in these answers, for I had no means of testing their correctness; but the woman seemed to speak unreservedly, and I am inclined to think that she said nothing but what, if necessary, could be substantiated. I spoke, also, to the young woman who was seated near her. She, like the others, was perfectly black, and appeared stout and healthy, of which some of the persons present assured themselves by feeling her arms and ankles, looking into her mouth, and causing her to stand up. She told me she had several brothers and sisters, but did not know where they were. She said she was a house-servant, and would be glad to be bought by a good master—looking at me, as if I should not be unacceptable.

I have said that there was an entire absence of emotion in the party of men, women, and children, thus seated preparatory to being sold. This does not correspond with the ordinary accounts of slave-sales, which are represented as tearful and harrowing. My belief is, that none of the parties felt deeply on the subject, or at least that any distress they experienced was but momentary—soon passed away, and was forgotten. One of my reasons for this opinion rests on a trifling incident which occurred. While waiting for the commencement of the sale, one of the gentlemen present amused himself with a pointer-dog, which, at command, stood on its hind-legs, and took pieces of bread from his pocket. These tricks greatly entertained the row of negroes, old and young; and the poor woman, whose heart three minutes before was almost broken, now laughed as heartily as any one.

Bidding Commences

"Sale is going to commence—this way, gentlemen," cried a man at the door to a number of loungers outside; and all having assembled, the mulatto assistant led the woman and her children to the block, which he helped her to mount. There she stood with her infant at the breast, and one of her girls at each side. The auctioneer, a handsome, gentlemanly personage, took his place, with one foot on an old deal-chair with a broken back, and the other raised on the somewhat more elevated block. It was a striking scene.

"Well, gentlemen," began the salesman, "here is a capital woman and her three children, all in good health—what do you say for them? Give me an offer. (Nobody speaks.) I put up the whole lot at 850 dollars—850 dollars—850 dollars (speaking very fast)—850 dollars. Will no one advance upon that? A very extraordinary bargain, gentlemen. A fine healthy baby. Hold it up. (Mulatto goes up the first step of the block; takes the baby from the woman's breast, and holds it aloft with one hand, so as to shew that it was a veritable sucking-baby.) That will do. A woman, still young, and three children, all for 850 dollars. An advance, if you please, gentlemen. (A voice bids 860.) Thank you, sir—860; any one bids more? (A second voice says, 870; and so on the bidding goes as far as 890 dollars, when it stops.) That won't do, gentlemen. I cannot take such a low price. (After a pause, addressing the mulatto): She may go down." Down from the block the woman and her children were therefore conducted by the assistant, and, as if nothing had occurred, they calmly resumed their seats by the stove.

The next lot brought forward was one of the men. The mulatto beckoning to him with his hand, requested him to come behind a canvas screen, of two leaves, which was standing near the back-window. The man placidly rose, and having been placed behind the screen, was ordered to take off his clothes, which he did without a word or look of remonstrance. About a dozen gentlemen crowded to the spot while the poor fellow was stripping himself, and as soon as he stood on the floor, bare from top to toe, a most rigorous scrutiny of his person was instituted. The clear black skin, back and front, was viewed all over for sores from disease; and there was no part of his body left unexamined. The man was told to open and shut his hands, asked if he could pick cotton, and every tooth in his head was scrupulously looked at. The investigation being at an end, he was ordered to dress himself; and having done so, was requested to walk to the block.

The ceremony of offering him for competition was gone through as before, but no one would bid. The other two men, after undergoing similar examinations behind the screen, were also put up, but with the same result. Nobody would bid for them, and they were all sent back to their seats. It seemed as if the company had conspired not to buy anything that day. Probably some imperfections had been detected in the personal qualities of the negroes. Be this as it may, the auctioneer, perhaps a little out of temper from his want of success, walked off to his desk, and the affair was so far at an end.

Migratory Bidders

"This way, gentlemen—this way!" was heard from a voice outside, and the company immediately hived off to the second establishment. At this office there was a young woman, and also a man, for sale. The woman was put up first at 500 dollars; and possessing some recommendable qualities, the bidding for her was run as high as 710 dollars, at which she was knocked down to a purchaser. The man, after the customary examination behind a screen, was put up at 700 dollars; but a small imperfection having been observed in his person, no one would bid for him; and he was ordered down.

"This way, gentlemen—this way, down the street, if you please!" was now shouted by a person in the employment of the first firm, to whose office all very willingly adjourned— one migratory company, it will be perceived, serving all the slave-auctions in the place. Mingling in the crowd, I went to see what should be the fate of the man and boy, with whom I had already had some communication.

There the pair, the two cousins, sat by the fire, just where I had left them an hour ago. The boy was put up first.

"Come along, my man—jump up; there's a good boy!" said one of the partners, a bulky and respectable-looking person, with a gold chain and bunch of seals; at the same time getting on the block. With alacrity the little fellow came forward, and, mounting the steps, stood by his side. The forms in front were filled by the company; and as I seated myself, I found that my old companion, Wide-awake, was close at hand, still chewing and spitting at a great rate.

Selling a Boy

"Now, gentlemen," said the auctioneer, putting his hand on the shoulder of the boy, "here is a very fine boy, seven years of age, warranted sound—what do you say for him? I put him up at 500 dollars—500 dollars (speaking quick, his right hand raised up, and coming down on the open palm of his left)—500 dollars. Any one say more than 500 dollars. (560 is bid.) 560 dollars. Nonsense! Just look at him. See how high he is. (He draws the lot in front of him, and shews that the little fellow's head comes up to his breast.) You see he is a fine, tall, healthy boy. Look at his hands."

Several step forward, and cause the boy to open and shut his hands—the flexibility of the small fingers, black on the one side, and whitish on the other, being well looked to. The hands, and also the mouth, having given satisfaction, an advance is made to 570, then to 580 dollars.

"Gentlemen, that is a very poor price for a boy of this size. (Addressing the lot): Go down, my boy, and shew them how you can run."

The boy, seemingly happy to do as he was bid, went down from the block, and ran smartly across the floor several times; the eyes of every one in the room following him.

"Now, that will do. Get up again. (Boy mounts the block, the steps being rather deep for his short legs; but the auctioneer kindly lends him a hand.) Come, gentlemen, you see this is a first-rate lot. (590—600—610—620—630 dollars are bid.) I will sell him for 630 dollars. (Right hand coming down on left.) Last call. 630 dollars once—630 dollars twice. (A pause; hand sinks.) Gone!"

The boy having descended, the man was desired to come forward; and after the usual scrutiny behind a screen, he took his place on the block.

'Well, now, gentlemen,' said the auctioneer, 'here is a right prime lot. Look at this man; strong, healthy, able-bodied; could not be a better hand for field-work. He can drive a wagon, or anything. What do you say for him? I offer the man at the low price of 800 dollars—he is well worth 1200 dollars. Come, make an advance, if you please. 800 dollars said for the man (a bid), thank you; 810 dollars— 810 dollars—810 dollars (several bids)—820—830—850— 860—going at 860—going. Gentlemen, this is far below his value. A strong-boned man, fit for any kind of heavy work. Just take a look at him. (Addressing the lot): Walk down. (Lot dismounts, and walks from one side of the shop to the other. When about to reascend the block, a gentleman, who is smoking a cigar, examines his mouth and his fingers. Lot resumes his place.) Pray, gentlemen, be quick (continues the auctioneer); I must sell him, and 860 dollars are only bid for the man—860 dollars. (A fresh run of bids to 945 dollars.) 945 dollars once, 945 dollars twice (looking slowly round, to see if all were done), 945 dollars, going—going (hand drops)—gone!'

A Curious Affair

During this remarkable scene, I sat at the middle of the front form, with my note-book in my hand, in order to obtain a full view of the transaction. So strange was the spectacle, that I could hardly dispel the notion that it was all a kind of dream; and now I look back upon the affair as by far the most curious I ever witnessed. The more intelligent Virginians will sympathise in my feelings on the occasion. I had never until now seen human beings sold; the thing was quite new. Two men are standing on an elevated bench, one white and the other black. The white man is auctioning the black man. What a contrast in look and relative position! The white is a most respectable-looking person; so far as dress is concerned, he might pass for a clergyman or churchwarden. There he stands—can I believe my eyes?—in the might of an Anglo-Saxon, sawing the air with his hand, as if addressing a missionary or any other philanthropic meeting from a platform. Surely that gentlemanly personage cannot imagine that he is engaged in any mortal sin! Beside him is a man with a black skin, and clothed in rough garments. His looks are downcast and submissive. He is being sold, just like a horse at Tattersall's, or a picture at Christie and Manson's [auction house]—I must be under some illusion. That dark object, whom I have been always taught to consider a man, is not a man. True, he may be called a man in advertisements, and by the mouth of auctioneers. But it is only a figure of speech—a term of convenience. He is a man in one sense, and not in another. He is a kind of man—stands upright on two legs, has hands to work, wears clothes, can cook his food (a point not reached by monkeys), has the command of speech, and, in a way, can think and act like a rational creature—can even be taught to read. But nature has thought fit to give him a black skin, and that tells very badly against him. Perhaps, also, there is something wrong with his craniological development. Being, at all events, so much of a man—genus *homo*—is it quite fair to master him, and sell him, exactly as suits your convenience—you being, from a variety of fortunate circumstances, his superior? All this passed through my mind as I sat on the front form in the saleroom of Messrs _____, while one of the members of that well-known firm was engaged in pursuing, by the laws of Virginia, his legitimate calling.

Such were a forenoon's experiences in the slave-market of Richmond. Everything is described precisely as it occurred, without passion or prejudice. It would not have been difficult to be sentimental on a subject which appeals so strongly to the feelings; but I have preferred telling the simple truth. In a subsequent chapter, I shall endeavour to offer some general views of slavery in its social and political relations.

Chapter 2

Foreign
Perspectives

Chapter Preface

A t first, African slaves made up a relatively small percentage of the population in the British colonies. Over time, the number of Africans and African Americans grew, and slaves came to occupy a distinctive class of their own, a class lying on the lowest rung on society's ladder. After the United States won its independence, the distinction between white laborers and black slaves hardened, as did the economic differences between the North and the South. A unique situation was developing in the New World, where the modern Industrial Revolution was developing hand in hand with one of the oldest and most backward institutions in human history.

In the home countries of Europe, where slavery was no longer practiced, the United States and slavery formed a popular topic of debate among social reformers, politicians, and journalists. The conditions of slavery also drew the strong interest of travelers from Europe and journalists from areas of the North where slavery had become a thing of the past. After all, Europe had just gone through the Enlightenment, a movement that propounded a democratic and scientific new spirit. The Enlightenment sparked a new interest in social conditions and a feeling that the world was going through revolutionary changes—plain to see in the British colonies, founded in individual liberty, as well as in France, home to one of the most powerful monarchies in the world before 1789.

In contrast, eyewitness accounts by Northern journalists often served less as inquiry than as propaganda. By revealing the harshness and violence of the slave system, editors sympathetic to abolitionism could advance their cause among the reading public, many of whom did not give slavery or the South much thought. Whether they were written by Europeans or Americans, however, eyewitness accounts of slavery all contained a fundamental, usually unspoken query: Could a country at the forefront of the Industrial Revolution, and representing the ideals of the Enlightenment, hold to an outmoded system of labor and survive?

A Redcoat's View of Plantation Life

Thomas Anburey

Lieutenant Thomas Anburey, a British officer serving under General John Burgoyne, was captured after the Battle of Saratoga, an early turning point of the Revolutionary War. Anburey's captors marched him from the Hudson Valley to Boston, then to Charlottesville, Virginia, where he remained a prisoner until the war's end. On his forced march Anburey had ample opportunity to observe the customs of American slave-holders. In the Chesapeake region, planters were discovering that staple crops were best grown on large plantations, where economies of scale allowed a much greater margin of profit. To work these plantations, however, large numbers of laborers were needed—and the only ready sources of such labor were the auction houses where Africans were offered for sale.

This plantation system gave rise to a rapid growth in the slavery business that would continue into the early nineteenth century and make the entire southern half of the United States dependent on forced labor. Anburey witnessed the beginning of this era in his book *Travels Through the Interior Parts of America,* which was published after his return to England in 1789.

The whole management of the plantation is left to the overseer, who as an encouragement to make the most of the crops, has a certain portion as his wages, but not having any interest in the negroes, any further than their labour, he drives and whips them about, and works them beyond

From Thomas Anburey, *Travels Through the Interior Parts of America* (Boston: 1923).

their strength, and sometimes till they expire; he feels no loss in their death, he knows the plantation must be supplied, and his humanity is estimated by his interest, which rises always above freezing point.

It is the poor negroes who alone work hard, and I am sorry to say, fare hard. Incredible is the fatigue which the poor wretches undergo, and that nature should be able to support it; there certainly must be something in their constitutions, as well as their color, different from us, that enables them to endure it.

They are called up at day break, and seldom allowed to swallow a mouthful of homminy [ground cornmeal], or hoe cake, but are drawn out into the field immediately, where they continue at hard labour, without intermission, till noon, when they go to their dinners, and are seldom allowed an hour for that purpose; their meals consist of homminy and salt [pork], and if their master is a man of humanity, touched by the finer feelings of love and sensibility, he allows them twice a week a little fat, skimmed milk, rusty bacon, or salt herring, to relish this miserable and scanty fare. The man at this plantation, in lieu of these, grants his negroes an acre of ground, and all Saturday afternoon to raise grain and poultry for themselves. After they have dined, they return to labour in the field, until dusk in the evening; here one naturally imagines the daily labour of these poor creatures was over, not so, they repair to the tobacco houses, where each has a task of stripping [tobacco leaves] allotted which takes them up some hours, or else they have such a quantity of Indian corn to husk, and if they neglect it, are tied up in the morning, and receive a number of lashes from those unfeeling monsters, the overseers, whose masters suffer them to exercise their brutal authority without constraint. Thus by their night task, it is late in the evening before these poor creatures return to their second scanty meal, and the time taken up at it encroaches upon their hours of sleep, which for refreshment of food and sleep together can never be reckoned to exceed eight.

When they lay themselves down to rest, their comforts are

equally miserable and limited, for they sleep on a bench, or on the ground, with an old scanty blanket, which serves them at once for bed and covering, their clothing is not less wretched, consisting of a shirt and trousers of coarse, thin, hard, hempen stuff, in the Summer, with an addition of a very coarse woollen jacket, breeches, and shoes in Winter. But since the [start of the Revolutionary] war, their masters, for they cannot get the clothing as usual, suffer them to go in rags, and many in a state of nudity.

The female slaves share labour and repose just in the same manner, except a few who are term'd house negroes, and are employed in household drudgery.

These poor creatures are all submission to injuries and insults, and are obliged to be passive, nor dare they resist or defend themselves if attacked, without the smallest provocation, by a white person, as the law directs the negroe's arm to be cut off who raises it against a white person, should it be only in defence against wanton barbarity and outrage.

Notwithstanding this humiliating state and rigid treatment to which this wretched race are subject, they are devoid of care, and appear jovial, contented, and happy. It is a fortunate circumstance that they possess, and are blessed with such an easy satisfied disposition, otherwise they must inevitably sink under such a complication of misery and wretchedness.

An Inhuman Institution

Hector St. John de Crèvecoeur

Born in Normandy as a member of the French nobility, Hector St. John de Crèvecoeur (born Michel-Guillaume Jean de Crèvecoeur) served in the French army that defended Quebec from the British during the French and Indian Wars. After the fall of Quebec, he moved south to the British colonies, where he took up farming, travel, and letter writing. During the five decades he spent in North America, Crèvecoeur had many opportunities to visit and observe the far-flung colonies, which held his interest for showing the strengths and weaknesses of a people taming a virgin land and benefitting from political liberty.

Crèvecoeur's "Letters" were a wide-ranging correspondence on colonial life first published in 1782. In one long and emotional passage, he describes the elegant life of Charleston, which in the colonial era was one of the wealthiest cities in North America. Crèvecoeur's admiration of the city was balanced by his exposure to the slavery that allowed local planters to prosper from trade in rice, indigo, and tobacco. Inspired by a terrifying encounter with one of slavery's victims, the author draws some bitter and cynical conclusions about humanity in general.

Charles-Town is, in the north, what Lima [Peru] is in the south; both are Capitals of the richest provinces of their respective hemispheres: you may therefore conjecture, that both cities must exhibit the appearances necessarily result-

From Hector St. John de Crèvecoeur, *Letters from an American Farmer* (London: J.M. Dent, 1912).

ing from riches. Peru abounding in gold, Lima is filled with inhabitants who enjoy all those gradations of pleasure, refinement, and luxury, which proceed from wealth. Carolina produces commodities, more valuable perhaps than gold, because they are gained by greater industry; it exhibits also on our northern stage, a display of riches and luxury, inferior indeed to the former, but far superior to what are to be seen in our northern towns. Its situation is admirable, being built at the confluence of two large rivers, which receive in their course a great number of inferior streams; all navigable in the spring, for flat boats. Here the produce of this extensive territory concentres; here therefore is the seat of the most valuable exportation; their wharfs, their docks, their magazines, are extremely convenient to facilitate this great commercial business. The inhabitants are the gayest in America; it is called the centre of our beau monde, and is always filled with the richest planters of the province, who resort hither in quest of health and pleasure. Here are always to be seen a great number of valetudinarians [invalids] from the West Indies, seeking for the renovation of health, exhausted by the debilitating nature of their sun, air, and modes of living. Many of these West Indians have I seen, at thirty, loaded with the infirmities of old age; for nothing is more common in those countries of wealth, than for persons to lose the abilities of enjoying the comforts of life, at a time when we northern men just begin to taste the fruits of our labour and prudence. The round of pleasure, and the expenses of those citizens' tables, are much superior to what you would imagine: indeed the growth of this town and province has been astonishingly rapid. It is pity that the narrowness of the neck on which it stands prevents it from increasing; and which is the reason why houses are so dear. The heat of the climate, which is sometimes very great in the interior parts of the country, is always temperate in Charles-Town; though sometimes when they have no sea breezes the sun is too powerful. The climate renders excesses of all kinds very dangerous, particularly those of the table; and yet, insensible or fearless of danger, they live on, and enjoy a short and a merry life: the rays of their sun seem to urge them irresistibly to dissipation and pleasure: on the contrary, the women, from being abstemious, reach to a longer period of life, and seldom die without having had several husbands. A European at his first arrival must be greatly surprised when he sees the elegance of their houses, their sumptuous furniture, as well as the magnificence of their tables. Can he imagine himself in a country, the establishment of which is so recent?. . .

A Very Different Life

While all is joy, festivity, and happiness in Charles-Town, would you imagine that scenes of misery overspread in the country? Their ears by habit are become deaf, their hearts are hardened; they neither see, hear, nor feel for the woes of their poor slaves, from whose painful labours all their wealth proceeds. Here the horrors of slavery, the hardship of incessant toils, are unseen; and no one thinks with compassion of those showers of sweat and of tears which from the bodies of Africans, daily drop, and moisten the ground they till. The cracks of the whip urging these miserable beings to excessive labour, are far too distant from the gay Capital to be heard. The chosen race eat, drink, and live happy, while the unfortunate one grubs up the ground, raises indigo, or husks the rice; exposed to a sun full as scorching as their native one; without the support of good food, without the cordials of any cheering liquor. This great contrast has often afforded me subjects of the most conflicting meditation. On the one side, behold a people enjoying all that life affords most bewitching and pleasurable, without labour, without fatigue, hardly subjected to the trouble of wishing. With gold, dug from Peruvian mountains, they order vessels to the coasts of Guinea; by virtue of that gold, wars, murders, and devastations are committed in some harmless, peaceable African neighbourhood, where dwelt innocent people, who even knew not but that all men were black. The daughter torn from her weeping mother, the child from the wretched parents, the wife from the loving husband; whole families swept away and brought through storms and tempests to this rich metropolis! There, arranged like horses at a fair, they are branded like cattle, and then driven to toil, to starve, and to languish for a few years on the different plantations of these citizens. And for whom must they work? For persons they know not, and who have no other power over them than that of violence, no other right than what this accursed metal [gold] has given them! Strange order of things! Oh, Nature, where art thou?—Are not these blacks thy children as well as we? On the other side, nothing is to be seen but the most diffusive misery and wretchedness, unrelieved even in thought or wish! Day after day they drudge on without any prospect of ever reaping for themselves; they are obliged to devote their lives, their limbs, their will, and every vital exertion to swell the wealth of masters; who look not upon

A Northerner Reconsiders

Many Northerners had their suspicions about and opposition to slavery confirmed by travel to the South. But not all. Nehemiah Adams, a Boston minister with abolitionist leanings, was pleasantly surprised by his journey southward. It seemed to him that slavery had positive effects on civic life and promoted the happiness of both races, results that Adams describes in his book A South-Side View of Slavery. *The book, which includes the following extract, became an important weapon for the pro-slavery faction in their ongoing battle for public support.*

Judging of them [slaves] as you meet them in the streets, see them at work, or at church, or in their prayer meetings and singing meetings, or walking on the Sabbath or holidays, one must see that they are a happy people, their physical condition superior to that of very many of our operatives, far superior to the common Irish people in our cities, and immeasurably above thousands in Great Britain. . . . It is obvious that if one can have all his present wants supplied, with no care about short crops, the markets, notes them with half the kindness and affection with which they consider their dogs and horses. Kindness and affection are not the portion of those who till the earth, who carry the burdens, who convert the logs into useful boards. This reward, simple and natural as one would conceive it, would border on humanity; and planters must have none of it!

Parenthood

If negroes are permitted to become fathers, this fatal indulgence only tends to increase their misery: the poor companions of their scanty pleasures are likewise the companions of their labours; and when at some critical seasons they could wish to see them relieved, with tears in their eyes they behold them perhaps doubly oppressed, obliged to bear the burden of nature—a fatal present—as well as that of un-

payable, bills due, be relieved from the necessity of planning and contriving, all the hard thinking being done for him by another, while useful and honorable employment fills his thoughts and hands, he is so far in a situation favorable to great comfort which will show itself in his whole outer man. Some will say, "This is the lowest kind of happiness." Yet it is all that a large portion of the race seek for; and few, except slaves, obtain it. Thus far I am constrained to say, that the relief which my feelings have experienced in going to the south and seeing the slaves at home is very great. Whatever else may be true of their condition, to whatever perils or sorrows, from causes not yet spoken of, they may be subjected, I feel like one who has visited a friend who is sick and reported to be destitute and extremely miserable, but has found him comfortable and happy. The sickness is there, but the patient is not only comfortable, but happy, if the ordinary proofs of it are to be taken. We may wonder that he should be; we may prove on paper that he can not be; but if the colored people of Savannah, Columbia, and Richmond are not, as a whole, a happy people, I have never seen any.

abated tasks. How many have I seen cursing the irresistible
propensity, and regretting, that by having tasted of those
harmless joys, they had become the authors of double misery to their wives. Like their masters, they are not permitted
to partake of those ineffable sensations with which nature
inspires the hearts of fathers and mothers; they must repel
them all, and become callous and passive. This unnatural
state often occasions the most acute, the most pungent of
their afflictions; they have no time, like us, tenderly to rear
their helpless off-spring, to nurse them on their knees, to enjoy the delight of being parents. Their paternal fondness is
embittered by considering, that if their children live, they
must live to be slaves like themselves; no time is allowed
them to exercise their pious office, the mothers must fasten
them on their backs, and, with this double load, follow their
husbands in the fields, where they too often hear no other
sound than that of the voice or whip of the taskmaster, and
the cries of their infants, broiling in the sun. These unfortunate creatures cry and weep like their parents, without a possibility of relief; the very instinct of the brute, so laudable,
so irresistible, runs counter here to their master's interest;
and to that god, all the laws of nature must give way. Thus
planters get rich; so raw, so unexperienced am I in this mode
of life, that were I to be possessed of a plantation, and my
slaves treated as in general they are here, never could I rest
in peace; my sleep would be perpetually disturbed by a retrospect of the frauds committed in Africa, in order to entrap
them; frauds surpassing in enormity everything which a
common mind can possibly conceive. I should be thinking
of the barbarous treatment they meet with on ship-board; of
their anguish, of the despair necessarily inspired by their situation, when torn from their friends and relations; when delivered into the hands of a people differently coloured,
whom they cannot understand; carried in a strange machine
over an ever agitated element, which they had never seen before; and finally delivered over to the severities of the whip-
pers, and the excessive labours of the field. Can it be possible that the force of custom should ever make me deaf to all

these reflections, and as insensible to the injustice of that trade, and to their miseries, as the rich inhabitants of this town seem to be? What then is man; this being who boasts so much of the excellence and dignity of his nature, among that variety of unscrutable mysteries, of unsolvable problems, with which he is surrounded? The reason why man has been thus created, is not the least astonishing! It is said, I know that they are much happier here than in the West Indies; because land being cheaper upon this continent than in those islands, the fields allowed them to raise their subsistence from, are in general more extensive. The only possible chance of any alleviation depends on the humour of the planters, who, bred in the midst of slaves, learn from the example of their parents to despise them; and seldom conceive either from religion or philosophy, any ideas that tend to make their fate less calamitous; except some strong native tenderness of heart, some rays of philanthropy, overcome the obduracy contracted by habit.

A Better Slavery

I have not resided here long enough to become insensible of pain for the objects which I every day behold. In the choice of my friends and acquaintance, I always endeavour to find out those whose dispositions are somewhat congenial with my own. We have slaves likewise in our northern provinces; I hope the time draws near when they will be all emancipated: but how different their lot, how different their situation, in every possible respect! They enjoy as much liberty as their masters, they are as well clad, and as well fed; in health and sickness they are tenderly taken care of; they live under the same roof, and are, truly speaking, a part of our families. Many of them are taught to read and write, and are well instructed in the principles of religion; they are the companions of our labours, and treated as such; they enjoy many perquisites, many established holidays, and are not obliged to work more than white people. They marry where inclination leads them; visit their wives every week; are as decently clad as the common people; they are indulged in educating, cherishing, and chastising their children, who are taught subordination to them as to their lawful parents: in short, they participate in many of the benefits of our society, without being obliged to bear any of its burdens. They are fat, healthy, and hearty, and far from repining at their fate; they think themselves happier than many of the lower class whites: they share with their masters the wheat and meat provision they help to raise; many of those whom the good Quakers have emancipated have received that great benefit with tears of regret, and have never quitted, though free, their former masters and benefactors.

Sensible Hearts

But is it really true, as I have heard it asserted here, that those blacks are incapable of feeling the spurs of emulation, and the cheerful sound of encouragement? By no means; there are a thousand proofs existing of their gratitude and fidelity: those hearts in which such noble dispositions can grow, are then like ours, they are susceptible of every generous sentiment, of every useful motive of action; they are capable of receiving lights, of imbibing ideas that would greatly alleviate the weight of their miseries. But what methods have in general been made use of to obtain so desirable an end? None; the day in which they arrive and are sold, is the first of their labours; labours, which from that hour admit of no respite; for though indulged by law with relaxation on Sundays, they are obliged to employ that time which is intended for rest, to till their little plantations. What can be expected from wretches in such circumstances? Forced from their native country, cruelly treated when on board, and not less so on the plantations to which they are driven; is there anything in this treatment but what must kindle all the passions, sow the seeds of inveterate resentment, and nourish a wish of perpetual revenge? They are left to the irresistible effects of those strong and natural propensities; the blows they receive, are they conducive to extinguish them, or to win their affections? They are neither soothed by the hopes that their slavery will ever terminate but with their lives; or yet encouraged by the goodness of their food, or the mildness of their treatment. The very hopes held out to mankind by religion, that consolatory system, so useful to the miserable, are never presented to them; neither moral nor physical means are made use of to soften their chains; they are left in their original and untutored state; that very state wherein the natural propensities of revenge and warm passions are so soon kindled. Cheered by no one single motive that can impel the will, or excite their efforts; nothing but terrors and punishments are presented to them; death is denounced if they run away; horrid delaceration [whipping] if they speak with their native freedom; perpetually awed by the terrible cracks of whips, or by the fear of capital punishments, while even those punishments often fail of their purpose.

Moral Questions

A clergyman settled a few years ago at George-Town, and feeling as I do now, warmly recommended to the planters, from the pulpit, a relaxation of severity; he introduced the benignity of Christianity, and pathetically made use of the admirable precepts of that system to melt the hearts of his congregation into a greater degree of compassion toward their slaves than had been hitherto customary; "Sir," said one of his hearers, "we pay you a genteel salary to read to us the prayers of the liturgy, and to explain to us such parts of the Gospel as the rule of the church directs; but we do not want you to teach us what we are to do with our blacks." The clergyman found it prudent to withhold any farther admonition. Whence this astonishing right, or rather this barbarous custom, for most certainly we have no kind of right beyond that of force? We are told, it is true, that slavery cannot be so repugnant to human nature as we at first imagine, because it has been practised in all ages, and in all nations: the Lacedemonians [ancient Spartans] themselves, those great assertors of liberty, conquered the Helotes with the design of making them their slaves; the Romans, whom we consider as our masters in civil and military policy, lived in the exercise of the most horrid oppression; they conquered to plunder and to enslave. What a hideous aspect the face of the earth must then have exhibited! Provinces, towns, districts, often depopulated! their inhabitants driven to Rome, the greatest market in the world, and there sold by thousands! The Roman dominions were tilled by the hands of unfortunate people, who had once been, like their victors, free, rich, and possessed of every benefit society can confer; until they became subject to the cruel right of war, and to lawless force. Is there then no superintending power who conducts the moral operations of the world, as well as the physical? The same sublime hand which guides the planets round the sun with so much exactness, which preserves the arrangement of the whole with such exalted wisdom and paternal care, and prevents the vast system from falling into confusion; doth it abandon mankind to all the errors, the follies, and the miseries, which their most frantic rage, and their most dangerous vices and passions can produce ?

The Nature of Mankind

The history of the earth! doth it present anything but crimes of the most heinous nature, committed from one end of the world to the other? We observe avarice, rapine, and murder, equally prevailing in all parts. History perpetually tells us of millions of people abandoned to the caprice of the maddest princes, and of whole nations devoted to the blind fury of tyrants. Countries destroyed; nations alternately buried in ruins by other nations; some parts of the world beautifully cultivated, returned again to the pristine state; the fruits of ages of industry, the toil of thousands in a short time destroyed by a few! If one corner breathes in peace for a few years, it is, in turn subjected, torn, and levelled; one would almost believe the principles of action in man, considered as the first agent of this planet, to be poisoned in their most essential parts. We certainly are not that class of beings which we vainly think ourselves to be; man an animal of prey, seems to have rapine and the love of bloodshed implanted in his heart; nay, to hold it the most honourable occupation in society: we never speak of a hero of mathematics, a hero of knowledge of humanity; no, this illustrious appellation is reserved for the most successful butchers of the world. If Nature has given us a fruitful soil to inhabit, she has refused us such inclinations and propensities as would afford us the full enjoyment of it. Extensive as the surface of this planet is, not one half of it is yet cultivated, not half replenished; she created man, and placed him either in the woods or plains, and provided him with passions which must for ever oppose his happiness; everything is submitted to the power of the strongest; men, like the elements, are always at war; the weakest yield to the most potent; force, subtlety, and malice, always triumph over unguarded honesty and simplicity. Benignity, moderation, and justice, are virtues adapted only to the humble paths of life: we love to talk of virtue and to admire its beauty, while in the shade of solitude and retirement; but when we step forth into active life, if it happen to be in competition with any passion or desire, do we observe it to prevail? Hence so many religious impostors have triumphed over the credulity of mankind, and have rendered their frauds the creeds of succeeding generations, during the course of many ages; until worn away by time, they have been replaced by new ones. Hence the most unjust war, if supported by the greatest force, always succeeds; hence the most just ones, when supported only by their justice, as often fail. Such is the ascendancy of power; the supreme arbiter of all the revolutions which we observe in this planet: so irresistible is power, that it often thwarts the tendency of the most forcible causes, and prevents their subsequent salutary effects, though ordained for the good of man by the Governor of the universe. Such is the perverseness of human nature; who can describe it in all its latitude? . . .

Bad Treatment

The following scene will I hope account for these melancholy reflections, and apologise for the gloomy thoughts with which I have filled this letter: my mind is, and always has been, oppressed since I became a witness to it. I was not long since invited to dine with a planter who lived three

miles from ———, where he then resided. In order to avoid
the heat of the sun, I resolved to go on foot, sheltered in a
small path, leading through a pleasant wood. I was leisure-
ly travelling along, attentively examining some peculiar
plants which I had collected, when all at once I felt the air
strongly agitated, though the day was perfectly calm and sul-
try. I immediately cast my eyes toward the cleared ground,
from which I was but at a small distance, in order to see
whether it was not occasioned by a sudden shower; when at
that instant a sound resembling a deep rough voice, uttered,
as I thought, a few inarticulate monosyllables. Alarmed and
surprised, I precipitately looked all round, when I perceived
at about six rods distance something resembling a cage, suspended to the limbs of a tree; all the branches of which appeared covered with large birds of prey, fluttering about, and
anxiously endeavouring to perch on the cage. Actuated by
an involuntary motion of my hands, more than by any design of my mind, I fired at them; they all flew to a short distance, with a most hideous noise: when, horrid to think and
painful to repeat, I perceived a negro, suspended in the cage,
and left there to expire! I shudder when I recollect that the
birds had already picked out his eyes, his cheek bones were
bare; his arms had been attacked in several places, and his
body seemed covered with a multitude of wounds. From the
edges of the hollow sockets and from the lacerations with
which he was disfigured, the blood slowly dropped, and
tinged the ground beneath. No sooner were the birds flown,
than swarms of insects covered the whole body of this unfortunate wretch, eager to feed on his mangled flesh and to
drink his blood. I found myself suddenly arrested by the
power of affright and terror; my nerves were convulsed; I
trembled, I stood motionless, involuntarily contemplating
the fate of this negro, in all its dismal latitude. The living
spectre, though deprived of his eyes, could still distinctly
hear, and in his uncouth dialect begged me to give him some
water to allay his thirst. Humanity herself would have re-
coiled back with horror; she would have balanced whether
to lessen such reliefless distress, or mercifully with one blow

to end this dreadful scene of agonising torture! Had I had a ball in my gun, I certainly should have despatched him; but finding myself unable to perform so kind an office, I sought, though trembling, to relieve him as well as I could. A shell ready fixed to a pole, which had been used by some negroes, presented itself to me; filled it with water, and with trembling hands I guided it to the quivering lips of the wretched sufferer. Urged by the irresistible power of thirst, he endeavoured to meet it, as he instinctively guessed its approach by the noise it made in passing through the bars of the cage. "Tankè, you whitè man, tankè you, putè somè poison and givè me." "How long have you been hanging there?" I asked him. "Two days, and me no die; the birds, the birds; aaah me!" Oppressed with the reflections which this shocking spectacle afforded me, I mustered strength enough to walk away, and soon reached the house at which I intended to dine. There I heard that the reason for this slave being thus punished, was on account of his having killed the overseer of the plantation. They told me that the laws of self-preservation rendered such executions necessary; and supported the doctrine of slavery with the arguments generally made use of to justify the practice; with the repetition of which I shall not trouble you at present.—Adieu.

Revolutionary Opinions

J.P. Brissot de Warville

J.P. Brissot de Warville published his *New Travels in the United States* in 1791, a time when he was fighting the dangerous battles of the French Revolution as a leader of the Girondin party. Like many other revolutionary leaders, de Warville took inspiration from the American colonists' successful fight for independence from England. But he also found a lesson to be drawn in the institution of slavery, which in his eyes degraded not only the slaves but also their owners. The principle of universal human liberty seemed to be reinforced by the native abilities of American slaves, who he found quite capable of the intellect and brilliance many whites and Europeans habitually reserved for other humans of their own color.

The French Revolution ended unhappily for de Warville and many others, however, as two years after his book appeared the author would fall from power and be executed on the guillotine.

In the four Northern [New England] states and in the Southern [Middle Atlantic] states, free Negroes are either domestic servants, small shopkeepers, or farmers. Some work on coasting vessels, but few dare to ship on long voyages because they are afraid of being carried off and sold in the West Indies.

Physically, these Negroes are in general vigorous. They have good constitutions, are able to perform the hardest la-

Reprinted by permission of the publisher from *New Travels in the United States of America, 1788*, by J.P. Brissot de Warville, translated by Mara Soceanu Vamos and Durand Echeverria, edited by Durand Echeverria (Cambridge, MA: Harvard University Press). Copyright © 1964 by the President and Fellows of Harvard College.

bor, and are generally active.[1] As servants, they are sober and faithful. All these traits are equally characteristic of Negro women. I have not seen any distinction made in respect to these qualities between Negro and white servants, though the latter always treat Negroes with contempt as if they belonged to an inferior race.

Those who are shopkeepers earn a moderate living but never expand their businesses beyond a certain point. The simple reason is that, although Negroes are everywhere treated humanely, the whites, who have the money, are not willing to lend a Negro the capital necessary for a big commercial establishment. Moreover, to succeed in a larger enterprise, a certain amount of preliminary experience is necessary and one must have had training in a countinghouse [i.e., business office]; but the forces of reason have not yet opened to Negroes the doors of countinghouses, in which they are not allowed to sit down alongside a white man. If, then, Negroes here are limited to the small retail trade, let us not attribute it to their lack of ability but rather to the prejudices of the whites, who put obstacles in their way.

For the same reasons Negroes in the country cannot own large farms. Their fields are small but usually well cultivated. European travelers are impressed by their good clothes, their well-kept log houses, and their many children, while the eye of the philosopher lingers with pleasure on these homes where tyranny causes no tears to flow.

In this part of America Negroes are certainly happy, but let us have the courage to admit that their happiness and their abilities have not reached the levels they are capable of attaining. There still is too great a distance between them and the whites, especially in the eye of public opinion, and this humiliating barrier frustrates all the efforts they make to elevate themselves. This discrimination is apparent everywhere. For instance, Negro children are admitted to public schools but they cannot cross the threshold of a college.

---

1. Married Negroes certainly have as many children as whites, but it has been observed that in cities the death rate of Negro children is higher. This difference is due not so much to their constitutions as to poverty, neglect, and particularly to lack of medical care.

They themselves, even though they are free and independent, are still in the habit of considering themselves inferior to the whites, who have rights they do not have.[2] Thus, it would not be fair to estimate the nature and extent of Negroes' abilities on the basis of the achievements of the free Negroes in the North.

The Southern Difference

Yet when we compare them with the slaves in the Southern states, what a tremendous difference we find! The brutalized and degraded condition of the latter is difficult to describe. Many are naked, underfed, and forced to sleep on straw in miserable huts.[3] They receive no education and no religious instruction whatsoever. They are not married, but coupled. The result is that they are brutish and lazy, lack energy, and have no ideas. They will not go to any trouble to get themselves clothes or better food, preferring to wear rags rather than mend them. Sunday, their day of rest, they spend doing absolutely nothing. Total inactivity is their supreme happiness, and as a consequence they do little work and perform their tasks listlessly.

In all fairness, I must admit that Southerners do not treat their slaves harshly; this is one of the effects of the general diffusion of the idea of liberty. Everywhere the slave works less, but that is all. Neither his food, nor his clothing, nor his morality, nor his thinking has improved; thus the master is the loser but the slave gains nothing. If Southerners followed

2. The aversion the whites have toward their daughters' marrying Negroes would in itself be enough to give a sense of humiliation. There are, however, a few examples of such marriages. In Pittsburgh there is a white woman of French origin who had been taken to London as a child and who at the age of twelve had been abducted by pirates who made a practice of kidnapping children and selling them in America for a fixed period of service. Through some strange circumstances this young woman married a Negro, who purchased her freedom and rescued her from a barbaric and libidinous white master who had made every effort to seduce her.   3. Dr. [Benjamin] Rush, who has had the opportunity to treat these Southern Negroes, shared with me a very important observation which proves how much the moral and intellectual energy of a man influences his health and physical condition. He told me that it is much more difficult to treat and to cure Negro slaves than white people and that the Negroes have much less resistance to serious and prolonged illnesses. This is so because they do not have the will to live; they are virtually without vitality and life force.

the example set by Northerners, both slaves and masters would benefit by the change.

In describing Negroes of the South, a careful distinction must be made between those who work in the fields and those who work as house servants. The preceding description applies only to the former; the others, few in number, are generally better clad, more energetic, and less ignorant.

Dr. Derham's Story

It has been popularly believed until recently that Negroes are intellectually inferior to whites. Even respectable writers have supported this theory. This prejudice is now beginning to disappear, and the Northern states can furnish examples to prove its falsity. I shall cite only two striking cases, the first proving that through education Negroes can be made fit for any profession, and the second showing that a Negro's brain can accomplish the most astonishing mathematical calculations and can, therefore, deal with all the sciences.

During my stay in Philadelphia I saw a Negro named James Derham, a doctor who practices in New Orleans. His life story, confirmed by several doctors, is as follows: He was born in a family in Philadelphia, in which he was taught to read and write, and instructed in the principles of Christianity. When a boy he was transferred by his master to the late Dr. John Kearsley, Jr. of Philadelphia,[4] who employed him to compound medicines and to administer them to his patients. Upon the death of Dr. Kearsley, he became (after passing through several hands) the property of Dr. George West, surgeon to the Sixteenth British Regiment, under whom, during the late war in America, he performed many of the menial duties of medicine. At the close of the war, he was sold by Dr. West to Dr. Robert Dove of New Orleans, who employed him as an assistant in his business, in which capacity he gained so much of his master's confidence and friendship that Dr. Dove consented to liberate him, after two

---

4. [Dr. John Kearsley was the founder of Christ Church Hospital in Philadelphia and helped draw the plans for Independence Hall.]

or three years, upon easy terms. By his numerous opportunities of improving in medicine Derham became so well acquainted with the healing art as to commence practicing in New Orleans with success. He is now about twenty-six years of age, has a wife but no children and does business to the amount of $3,000, or about 16,000 livres, a year.

"I conversed with him," Dr. Wistar told me, "upon the acute and epidemic diseases of the country where he lives and found him perfectly acquainted with the modern simple mode of practice in these diseases. I expected to have suggested some new medicines to him; but he suggested many more to me." He is very modest and engaging in his manners. He speaks French fluently and has some knowledge of the Spanish language. By some accident, although born in a religious family, he was not baptized in his infancy, in consequence of which he applied to Dr. Withe [White] to receive baptism. He found him qualified, both by knowledge and moral conduct, to be admitted to baptism.

The Math Master

The other case was reported to me by Dr. Rush, a famous doctor and writer of Philadelphia, who has published an account of it.[5] Several of the details have since been confirmed by the wife of the immortal Washington, in whose neighborhood this Negro has long been living.

Thomas Fuller was born in Africa and can neither read nor write. He is now seventy years old and has lived all his life on Mrs. Cox's plantation, four miles from Alexandria. Two gentlemen, natives of Pennsylvania, Messrs. [William H.] Hartshorne and Samuel Coates, having heard in traveling in Virginia of his extraordinary powers in arithmetic, sent for him, and had their curiosity sufficiently gratified by the answers which he gave to the following questions:

First. Upon being asked how many seconds there are in a year and a half, he answered, in about two minutes, 47,304,000,

---

5. This doctor is also famous in America for his excellent political writings. He is an indefatigable apostle of liberty.

counting 365 days in the year.

Second. On being asked how many seconds a man has lived who is seventy years, seventeen days and twelve hours old, he answered, in a minute and a half, 2,210,500,800. One of the gentlemen, who employed himself with his pen in making these calculations, told him he was wrong, and that the sum was not so great as he said. This was true, because Fuller had overlooked the leap years, but with the greatest speed he corrected his figures.[6]

Third. Suppose a farmer has six sows and each sow has six female pigs the first year, and they all increase in the same proportion to the end of eight years, how many sows will the farmer then have? In ten minutes, he answered 34,588,806. The difference of time between his answering this and the two former questions was occasioned by a trifling mistake he had made from a misapprehension of the question.

After he had correctly answered all the questions, he told how he had discovered and developed his arithmetical talent. He began his application to figures by counting ten, and then when he was able to count a hundred, he thought himself (to use his own words) "a very clever fellow." He next amused himself counting, grain by grain, a bushel of wheat. From this he was led to calculate how many rails were necessary to enclose and how many grains of corn were necessary to sow a certain quantity of ground. From this application of his talents his mistress has often derived considerable benefit, and he spoke of her with great respect and mentioned in a particular manner his obligations to her for refusing to sell him, which she had been tempted to do by offers of large sums of money. He said his memory was beginning to fail him. When one of the gentlemen remarked in his presence that it was a pity he had not had an education equal to his genius, he said: "No, massa, it is best I got no learning; for many learned men be great fools."

6. [We have translated the last sentence as Brissot wrote it, but he had misunderstood the English original, which read: ". . . not so great as he said–upon which the old man hastily replied, 'Top, massa, you forget de leap year.' On adding the seconds of the leap years to the others, the amount of the whole in both their sums agreed exactly." *American Museum.*]

The Stamp of Slavery

These examples prove beyond a doubt that the mental capacity of Negroes is equal to any task, and that all they need is education and freedom. The difference between those who are free and educated and those who are not can also be seen in their work. The lands of both whites and Negroes in the free states, as for example in Connecticut or Pennsylvania, are infinitely better cultivated, produce larger crops, and present in general an impression of well-being and contentment. But cross over into Maryland and Virginia, and, as I have said before, you think you are in a different world. No longer will you see well-cultivated fields, neat and even elegant farmhouses, large, well-designed barns, and big herds of fat, healthy cattle. Everything in Maryland and in Virginia bears the stamp of slavery: the parched soil, the badly managed farming, the ramshackled houses, and the few scrawny cat-

---

Jefferson's Thoughts on Race

Slavery's historians have always paid close attention to the ideas and the actions of Thomas Jefferson, author of the Declaration of Independence and the third president of the United States. Jefferson placed himself squarely in the mainstream of Enlightenment thought as practiced by Europe's leading writers and philosophers. He believed that a rational, scientific examination of social problems would bring about understanding and solutions. In this manner, Jefferson first considered the question of slavery by examining the differences between white and black people, as follows in his Notes on the State of Virginia.

To our reproach it must be said, that though for a century and a half we have had under our eyes the races of black and of red men, they have never yet been viewed by us as subjects of natural history. I advance it, therefore, as a suspicion only, that the blacks, whether originally a distinct race, or made distinct by time and circumstances, are

tle that look like walking skeletons. In short, you find real poverty existing alongside a false appearance of wealth.

Even in the Southern states men are beginning to see that it is poor economy to feed a slave badly, and that capital invested in slaves does not pay its interest. The introduction of free labor into a part of Virginia, in the area along the lovely Shenandoah River, may be due more to these considerations and particularly to the economic impossibility of importing more slaves than to humanitarian motives. When you see the Shenandoah you think you are still in Pennsylvania.

Let us hope that all of Virginia will look like this in the perhaps not distant future, when it is no longer sullied by slavery. There are slaves in Virginia only because it is believed that they are necessary for raising tobacco. But this crop is decreasing every day in this state and will continue to decrease. The tobacco grown near the Ohio and Mississippi is

---

inferior to the whites in the endowments both of body and mind. It is not against experience to suppose that different species of the same genus, or varieties of the same species, may possess different qualifications. Will not a lover of natural history then, one who views the gradations in all the races of animals with the eye of philosophy, excuse an effort to keep those in the department of man as distinct as nature has formed them? This unfortunate difference of color, and perhaps of faculty, is a powerful obstacle to the emancipation of these people. Many of their advocates, while they wish to vindicate the liberty of human nature, are anxious also to preserve its dignity and beauty. Some of these, embarrassed by the question, "What further is to be done with them?" join themselves in opposition [to emancipation] with those who are actuated by sordid avarice only. Among the Romans emancipation required but one effort. The slave, when made free, might mix with, without staining the blood of his master. But with us a second [effort] is necessary, unknown to history. When freed, he is to be removed beyond the reach of mixture.

infinitely more plentiful, of better quality, and requires less labor. When it finds an outlet to the European market, Virginians will be forced to abandon this crop and raise instead wheat, potatoes, and cattle. Intelligent Virginians are anticipating this change and are beginning to grow wheat.

General Washington Speaks

Chief among them must be listed that astonishing man who, though a beloved general, had the courage to be a sincere republican and who is the only one not to remember his own glory, a hero whose unique destiny it will be to save his country twice and to open for it the road to prosperity after having set it on the road to liberty. Now *wholly* occupied with improving his land, developing new crops, and building roads, he is giving to his fellow citizens a useful example which will no doubt be followed. Nevertheless he does own, I am forced to say, large numbers of Negro slaves. They are, however, most humanely treated. Well fed, well clothed, and required to do only a moderate amount of work, they continually bless the master God gave them. It would undoubtedly be fitting that such a lofty, pure, and disinterested soul be the one to make the first step in the abolition of slavery in Virginia. This great man, when I had the honor to talk with him, told me that he admired everything that was being done in the other states and that he desired the extension of the movement in his own. But he did not conceal the fact that there are still many obstacles and that it would be dangerous to make a frontal attack on a prejudice which is beginning to decrease. "Time, patience, and education," he said, "and it will be overcome. Nearly all Virginians," he added, "are convinced that the general emancipation of Negroes cannot occur in the near future, and for this reason they do not wish to organize a society which might give their slaves dangerous ideas." Another obstacle which he pointed out is that most of this part of the country is made up of large plantations and people live far apart, so that it is difficult to hold meetings.

"Virginians are wrong," I told him. "It is evident that sooner or later Negroes will win their freedom everywhere, and that this revolution will extend to Virginia. It is therefore to the interest of your fellow citizens to prepare for it and to try to reconcile the restitution of the Negroes' rights with their own right to property. The necessary steps can only be worked out by a society, and it would be fitting that the savior of America be its head and restore liberty to 300,000 unhappy inhabitants of his country." This great man told me that he was in favor of the formation of such a society and that he would support it, but that he did not believe the moment was favorable. No doubt there were greater problems which demanded his attention and preoccupied him at the time; America's destiny was about to be placed a second time in his hands [i.e., he was about to be elected the first president].

Abolitionist Zeal

It is certainly a misfortune that no such society exists in Maryland or Virginia, for it is to the constant zeal of those in Philadelphia and New York that we owe the progress of this revolution in America and the birth of the society in London.

Would that I were able here to describe to you the impressions that crowded upon me as I attended the meetings of these three societies! How earnest were the faces of the members! How simple were their speeches! How frank were their discussions! What benevolence! What strength in their resolution! Everyone was eager to take part, not in order to shine, but in order to be of use. How great was their joy when they learned that a society similar to theirs was being formed in Paris, in that immense capital, so famous in America for its opulence, for its pomp, and for its influence over a vast kingdom and over almost all the states of Europe! How quickly did they publish this news in all their gazettes and circulate everywhere the translation of the first speech read before the Paris society. How great was their joy when they saw on the list of members of that society a name dear to their hearts, one which they pronounce only with affection [the Marquis de Lafayette], as well as the names of other persons known for their energy and patriotism! They were certain that if this society grew, if it faced the obstacles bravely, and if it united with the London society, then the information spread by these two groups on the slave trade and its unprofitable infamy would enlighten governments and persuade them to suppress the traffic.

It was no doubt this enthusiasm, and also the flattering recommendations I had brought with me from Europe, rather than my own feeble achievements, which won me the honor of being elected a member of these societies. They did not however limit themselves merely to words and gestures of support; they appointed committees to assist me in my work and opened their archives to me.

These beneficent societies are at present engaged in new projects to achieve their humanitarian ends and are endeavoring to create new societies in the states where there are none, as in Delaware, where one has just been organized. They are also working on new ways to discourage slavery and the slave trade. For example, in order to put a stop to the shameful public auctions of slaves still held in the state of New York, all members have undertaken never to employ the services of any public auctioneer who presides over such sales. The Philadelphia society is particularly ingenious in rescuing slaves from the hands of rapacious owners who have no right to hold them. If a slave is mistreated by his master, the society provides him with sure and free protection. If a slave has completed his time of servitude and is still detained by his master, the society demands that his rights be respected. Should strangers bring Negroes into the state and not comply with the provisions of the law, the society sees to it that these poor Negroes receive the legal benefits to which they are entitled. One of the best-known lawyers in Philadelphia, whose talents I admire and of whose friendship I am very proud, Mr. Miers Fisher, donates his services to the society and is almost always successful in the cases he undertakes. The society, having observed that many associations become ineffective because they become too large, has formed several committees which function permanently. It encourages the organization of similar committees in all the states to press for the enforcement of the laws forbidding the slave trade and regulating the freeing of slaves, and to keep submitting to the legislatures petitions for new laws to meet unforeseen cases. I have no doubt that the activities of this society will eventually lead to the formation of similar societies in the South.

Chapter 3

A Life in Bondage

Chapter Preface

A wide variety of occupations were forced on slave laborers in America. In the North, many slaves worked as house servants, in small factories or artisans' shops, or on small farms. In the South, the majority of slaves lived on farming estates. Most were agricultural laborers, giving their daylight hours to the cultivation of crops grown and harvested for sale to the North or abroad. Others worked as personal servants within Southern households. This system gave rise to a unique class division among slaves living in North America. House slaves were considered, both by masters and by other slaves, as quite different in ability and personality from those who worked outside.

No matter how they lived, all slaves were marked by their accent, skin color, and culture as completely alien to the white society that surrounded them. They lived apart and in constant fear of both physical punishment and the torment of having their families broken up and their loved ones sold to some distant place across the state or in another part of the country. They also suffered under the tyranny of masters whose whims and cruelty went unchecked by any law. They were property, pure and simple, and had no legal rights whatsoever. Although a few attained their freedom, most had little or no expectation for a better life.

Their lives may have been desperate and hopeless, but some slaves did succeed in recording their experiences, either by their own hand or through an interviewer. The slave narratives of the nineteenth century turned out to be one of the most popular literary genres of the time. They served a larger purpose, however, than merely selling books and magazines: They proved crucial in turning public attitudes against slavery and in favor of the abolitionist struggle.

The Uncertainties of Courtship and Marriage

Henry Bibb

> Under the watchful eye of masters and overseers, slaves carried on as best they could not only their assigned work but also a personal life of courtship, marriage, and child-rearing. But their legal status as personal property brought constant interference from their owners, who assumed the right to decide whom they would marry, when they would be married, and what would be done with their children.
>
> In one famous nineteenth-century slave autobiography, Henry Bibb describes the problems he faced while engaged to his young sweetheart, the property of a different owner, and the anguish of helplessness he suffered while witnessing the abuse of his wife and later his own children.

The circumstances of my courtship and marriage, I consider to be among the most remarkable events of my life while a slave. To think that after I had determined to carry out the great idea which is so universally and practically acknowledged among all the civilized nations of the earth, that I would be free or die, I suffered myself to be turned aside by the fascinating charms of a female, who gradually won my attention from an object so high as that of liberty; and an object which I held paramount to all others.

But when I had arrived at the age of eighteen, which was

From *Narrative of the Life and Adventures of Henry Bibb, an American Slave,* written by himself (New York: 1850).

in the year of 1833, it was my lot to be introduced to the favor of a mulatto slave girl named Malinda, who lived in Oldham County, Kentucky, about four miles from the residence of my owner. Malinda was a medium sized girl, graceful in her walk, of an extraordinary make, and active in business. Her skin was of a smooth texture, red cheeks, with dark and penetrating eyes. She moved in the highest circle[1] of slaves, and free people of color. She was also one of the best singers I ever heard, and was much esteemed by all who knew her, for her benevolence, talent and industry. In fact, I considered Malinda to be equalled by few, and surpassed by none, for the above qualities, all things considered.

A Union of Feeling

It is truly marvellous to see how sudden a man's mind can be changed by the charms and influence of a female. The first two or three visits that I paid this dear girl, I had no intention of courting or marrying her, for I was aware that such a step would greatly obstruct my way to the land of liberty. I only visited Malinda because I liked her company, as a highly interesting girl. But in spite of myself, before I was aware of it, I was deeply in love; and what made this passion so effectual and almost irresistable, I became satisfied that it was reciprocal. There was a union of feeling, and every visit made the impression stronger and stronger. One or two other young men were paying attention to Malinda, at the same time; one of whom her mother was anxious to have her marry. This of course gave me a fair opportunity of testing Malinda's sincerity. I had just about opposition enough to make the subject interesting. That Malinda loved me above all others on earth, no one could deny. I could read it by the warm reception with which the dear girl always met me, and treated me in her mother's house. I could read it by the warm and affectionate shake of the hand, and gentle smile upon her lovely cheek. I could read it by her al-

1. The distinction among slaves is as marked, as the classes of society are in any aristocratic community. Some refusing to associate with others whom they deem beneath them in point of character, color, condition, or the superior importance of their respective masters.

ways giving me the preference of her company; by her pressing invitations to visit even in opposition to her mother's will. I could read it in the language of her bright and sparkling eye, penciled by the unchangeable finger of nature, that spake but could not lie. These strong temptations gradually diverted my attention from my actual condition and from liberty, though not entirely.

But oh! that I had only then been enabled to have seen as I do now, or to have read the following slave code, which is but a stereotyped law of American slavery. It would have saved me I think from having to lament that I was a husband and am the father of slaves who are still left to linger out their days in hopeless bondage. The laws of Kentucky, my native State, with Maryland and Virginia, which are said to be the mildest slave States in the Union, noted for their humanity, Christianity and democracy, declare that "Any slave, for rambling in the night, or riding horseback without leave, or running away, may be punished by whipping, cropping and branding in the cheek, or otherwise, not rendering him unfit for labor." "Any slave convicted of petty larceny, murder, or wilfully burning of dwelling houses, may be sentenced to have his right hand cut off; to be hanged in the usual manner, or the head severed from the body, the body divided into four quarters, and head and quarters stuck up in the most public place in the county, where such act was committed."

Calling on Malinda

At the time I joined my wife in holy wedlock, I was ignorant of these ungodly laws; I knew not that I was propogating victims for this kind of torture and cruelty. Malinda's mother was free, and lived in Bedford, about a quarter of a mile from her daughter; and we often met and passed off the time pleasantly. Agreeable to promise, on one Saturday evening, I called to see Malinda, at her mother's residence, with an intention of letting her know my mind upon the subject of marriage. It was a very bright moonlight night; the dear girl was standing in the door, anxiously waiting my arrival. As I approached the door she caught my hand with an affectionate smile, and bid me welcome to her mother's fireside. After having broached the subject of marriage, I informed her of the difficulties which I conceived to be in the way of our marriage; and that I could never engage myself to marry any girl only on certain conditions; near as I can recollect the substance of our conversation upon the subject, it was, that I was religiously inclined; that I intended to try to comply with the requisitions of the gospel, both theoretically and practically through life. Also that I was decided on becoming a free man before I died; and that I expected to get free by running away, and going to Canada, under the British Government. Agreement on those two cardinal questions I made my test for marriage.

I said, "I never will give my heart nor hand to any girl in marriage, until I first know her sentiments upon the all-important subjects of Religion and Liberty. No matter how well I might love her, nor how great the sacrifice in carrying out these God-given principles. And I here pledge myself from this course never to be shaken while a single pulsation of my heart shall continue to throb for Liberty." With this idea Malinda appeared to be well pleased, and with a smile she looked me in the face and said, "I have long entertained the same views, and this has been one of the greatest reasons why I have not felt inclined to enter the married state while a slave; I have always felt a desire to be free; I have long cherished a hope that I should yet be free, either by purchase or running away. In regard to the subject of Religion, I have always felt that it was a good thing, and something that I would seek for at some future period." After I found that Malinda was right upon these all important questions, and that she truly loved me well enough to make me an affectionate wife, I made proposals for marriage. She very modestly declined answering the question then, considering it to be one of a grave character, and upon which our future destiny greatly depended. And notwithstanding she confessed that I had her entire affections, she must have some time to consider the matter. To this I of course consented, and was to meet her on the next Saturday night to decide the question. But for some cause I failed to come, and the next week she sent for me, and on the Sunday evening following I called on her again; she welcomed me with all the kindness of an affectionate lover, and seated me by her side. We soon broached the old subject of marriage, and entered upon a conditional contract of matrimony, viz: that we would marry if our minds should not change within one year; that after marriage we would change our former course and live a pious life; and that we would embrace the earliest opportunity of running away to Canada for our liberty. Clasping each other by the hand, pledging our sacred honor that we would be true, we called on high heaven to witness the rectitude of our purpose. There was nothing that could be more binding upon us as slaves than this; for marriage among American slaves, is disregarded by the laws of this country. It is counted a mere temporary matter; it is a union which may be continued or broken off, with or without the consent of a slaveholder, whether he is a priest or a libertine.

The Laws of Marriage

There is no legal marriage among the slaves of the South; I never saw nor heard of such a thing in my life, and I have been through seven of the slave states. A slave marrying according to law, is a thing unknown in the history of American Slavery. And be it known to the disgrace of our country that every slaveholder, who is the keeper of a number of slaves of both sexes, is also the keeper of a house or houses of ill-fame. Licentious white men, can and do, enter at night or day the lodging places of slaves; break up the bonds of affection in families; destroy all their domestic and social union for life; and the laws of the country afford them [slaves] no protection. Will any man count, if they can be counted, the churches of Maryland, Kentucky, and Virginia, which have slaves connected with them, living in an open state of adultery, never having been married according to the laws of the State, and yet regular members of these various denominations, but more especially the Baptist and Methodist church-es? And I hazard nothing in saying, that this state of things exists to a very wide extent in the above states.

I am happy to state that many fugitive slaves, who have been enabled by the aid of an over-ruling providence to escape to the free North with those whom they claim as their wives, notwithstanding all their ignorance and superstition, are not at all disposed to live together like brutes, as they have been compelled to do in slaveholding Churches. But as soon as they get free from slavery they go before some anti-slavery clergyman, and have the solemn ceremony of marriage performed according to the laws of the country. And if they profess religion, and have been baptized by a slaveholding minister, they repudiate it after becoming free, and are rebaptized by a man who is worthy of doing it according to the gospel rule.

Opponents

The time and place of my marriage, I consider one of the most trying of my life. I was opposed by friends and foes; my mother opposed me because she thought I was too young, and marrying she thought would involve me in trouble and difficulty. My mother-in-law opposed me, because she wanted her daughter to marry a slave who belonged to a very rich man living near by, and who was well known to be the son of his master. She thought no doubt that his master or father might chance to set him free before he died, which would enable him to do a better part by her daughter than I could! And there was no prospect then of my ever being free. But his master has neither died nor yet set his son free, who is now about forty years of age, toiling under the lash, waiting and hoping that his master may die and will him to be free.

The young men were opposed to our marriage for the same reason that Paddy opposed a match when the clergy-man was about to pronounce the marriage ceremony of a young couple. He said "if there be any present who have any objections to this couple being joined together in holy wed-

lock, let them speak now, or hold their peace henceforth."
At this time Paddy sprang to his feet and said, "Sir, I object
to this." Every eye was fixed upon him. "What is your ob-

Recollections of Virginia

The former slave Austin Steward, in his book Twenty-Two
Years a Slave and Forty Years a Freeman, *bitterly reflects
on his memories of a childhood in bondage.*

Now, after the lapse of so many years, when my
thoughts wander back, as they often do, to my native
State, I confess that painful recollections drive from my
mind those joyful emotions that should ever arise in the
heart of man, when contemplating the familiar scenes of
his youth, and especially when recurring to the venerable
shades and the sheltering roof under which he was born.
True, around the well-remembered spot where our childhood's years were spent, recollection still loves to linger;
yet memory, ever ready with its garnered store, paints in
glowing colors, Virginia's crouching slaves in the fore-
ground. Her loathsome slave-pens and slave markets—
chains, whips and instruments of torture; and back of all
this is as truthfully recorded the certain doom, the ret-
ributive justice, that will sooner or later overtake her; and
with a despairing sigh I turn away from the imaginary
view of my native State.

What though she may have been justly styled, "The
Mother of Presidents?" What avails the honor of being the
birth-place of the brave and excellent [George] Washington, while the prayers and groans of the down-trodden
African daily ascend to heaven for redress? What though
her soil be fertile, yielding a yearly product of wealth to its
possessors? And what matter is it, that their lordly mansions
are embowered in the shade of trees of a century's growth,
if, through their lofty and tangled branches, we espy the
rough cabin of the mangled bondman, and know that the
soil on which he labors has drunk his heart's blood?

jection?" said the clergyman. "Faith," replied Paddy, "Sir I want her myself."

The man to whom I belonged was opposed, because he feared my taking off from his farm some of the fruits of my own labor for Malinda to eat, in the shape of pigs, chickens, or turkeys, and would count it not robbery. So we formed a resolution, that if we were prevented from joining in wedlock, that we would run away, and strike for Canada, let the consequences be what they might. But we had one consolation; Malinda's master was very much in favor of the match, but entirely upon selfish principles. When I went to ask his permission to marry Malinda, his answer was in the affirmative with but one condition, which I consider to be too vulgar to be written in this book. Our marriage took place one night during the Christmas holidays; at which time we had quite a festival given us. All appeared to be wide awake, and we had quite a jolly time at my wedding party. And notwithstanding our marriage was without license or sanction of law, we believed it to be honorable before God, and the bed undefiled. Our Christmas holidays were spent in matrimonial visiting among our friends, while it should have been spent in running away to Canada, for our liberty. But freedom was little thought of by us, for several months after marriage. I often look back to that period even now as one of the most happy seasons of my life; notwithstanding all the contaminating and heartrending features with which the horrid system of slavery is marked, and must carry with it to its final grave, yet I still look back to that season with sweet remembrance and pleasure, that yet hath power to charm and drive back dull cares which have been accumulated by a thousand painful recollections of slavery. Malinda was to me an affectionate wife. She was with me in the darkest hours of adversity. She was with me in sorrow, and joy, in fasting and feasting, in trial and persecution, in sickness and health, in sunshine and in shade.

Sold to Mr. Gatewood

Some months after our marriage, the unfeeling master to whom I belonged sold his farm with the view of moving his slaves to the State of Missouri, regardless of the separation of husbands and wives forever; but for fear of my resuming my old practice of running away, if he should have forced me to leave my wife, by my repeated requests, he was constrained to sell me to his brother, who lived within seven miles of Wm. Gatewood, who then held Malinda as his property. I was permitted to visit her only on Saturday nights, after my work was done, and I had to be at home before sunrise on Monday mornings or take a flogging. He proved to be so oppressive, and so unreasonable in punishing his victims, that I soon found that I should have to run away in self-defence. But he soon began to take the hint, and sold me to Wm. Gatewood the owner of Malinda. With my new residence I confess that I was much dissatisfied. Not that Gatewood was a more cruel master than my former owner—not that I was opposed to living with Malinda, who was then the centre and object of my affections—but to live where I must be eye witness to her insults, scourgings and abuses, such as are common to be inflicted upon slaves, was more than I could bear. If my wife must be exposed to the insults and licentious passions of wicked slave-drivers and overseers; if she must bear the stripes of the lash laid on by an unmerciful tyrant; if this is to be done with impunity, which is frequently done by slaveholders and their abettors, Heaven forbid that I should be compelled to witness the sight.

Father of a Slave

Not many months after I took up my residence on Wm. Gatewood's plantation, Malinda made me a father. The dear little daughter was called Mary Frances. She was nurtured and caressed by her mother and father, until she was large enough to creep over the floor after her parents, and climb up by a chair before I felt it to be my duty to leave my family and go into a foreign country for a season. Malinda's business was to labor out in the field the greater part of her time, and there was no one to take care of poor little Frances, while her mother was toiling in the field. She was left at the house to creep under the feet of an unmerciful old mistress, whom I have known to slap with her hand the face of little Frances, for crying after her mother, until her little face was left black and blue. I recollect that Malinda and myself came from the field one summer's day at noon, and poor little Frances came creeping to her mother smiling, but with large tear drops standing in her dear little eyes, sobbing and trying to tell her mother that she had been abused, but was not able to utter a word. Her little face was bruised black with the whole print of Mrs. Gatewood's hand. This print was plainly to be seen for eight days after it was done. But oh! this darling child was a slave; born of a slave mother. Who can imagine what could be the feelings of a father and mother, when looking upon their infant child whipped and tortured with impunity, and they placed in a situation where they could afford it no protection. But we were all claimed and held as property; the father and mother were slaves!

On this same plantation I was compelled to stand and see my wife shamefully scourged and abused by her master; and the manner in which this was done, was so violently and inhumanly committed upon the person of a female, that I despair in finding decent language to describe the bloody act of cruelty. My happiness or pleasure was then all blasted; for it was sometimes a pleasure to be with my little family even in slavery. I loved them as my wife and child. Little Frances was a pretty child; she was quiet, playful, bright, and interesting. She had a keen black eye, and the very image of her mother was stamped upon her cheek; but I could never look upon the dear child without being filled with sorrow and fearful apprehensions, of being separated by slaveholders, because she was a slave, regarded as property. And unfortunately for me, I am the father of a slave, a word too obnoxious to be spoken by a fugitive slave. It calls fresh to my mind the separation of husband and wife; of stripping, tying up and flogging; of tearing children from their parents, and selling them on the auction block. It calls to mind female virtue trampled under foot with impunity. But oh! when I remember that my daughter, my only child, is still there, destined to share the fate of all these calamities, it is too much to bear. If ever there was any one act of my life while a slave, that I have to lament over it is that of being a father and a husband of slaves. I have the satisfaction of knowing that I am only the father of one slave. She is bone of my bone, and flesh of my flesh; poor unfortunate child. She was the first and shall be the last slave that ever I will father, for chains and slavery on this earth.

The Cruel Fate of Women

Harriet Jacobs

The condition of women under slavery could be doubly cruel.
They were held in bondage not only for their labor but also,
frequently, for their use as sexual servants. Many mulatto
children were born to southern slaveowners, who had no legal
obligation to recognize them as their own and who frequently
sold them to avoid any further trouble.

Born in Edenton, North Carolina, in 1813, Harriet Jacobs
was sold at the age of twelve to Dr. James Norcom. In 1834,
and after teaching herself to read and write, she escaped to
Philadelphia. After moving to New York, she set down her
memories of her life as a slave. Her straightforward description of bad treatment at the hands of Dr. Norcom (whose
name she changed to Dr. Flint) scandalized the northern public while appearing in serial form in the *New York Tribune*.
When it was finally published as a book in 1861, *Incidents in
the Life of a Slave Girl* became a best-seller.

During the first years of my service in Dr. Flint's family, I was accustomed to share some indulgences with
the children of my mistress. Though this seemed to me no
more than right, I was grateful for it, and tried to merit the
kindness by the faithful discharge of my duties. But I now
entered on my fifteenth year—a sad epoch in the life of a
slave girl. My master began to whisper foul words in my ear.
Young as I was, I could not remain ignorant of their import.

From Harriet Jacobs, *Incidents in the Life of a Slave Girl*, edited by L. Maria Child
(Boston: 1861).

I tried to treat them with indifference or contempt. The master's age, my extreme youth, and the fear that his conduct would be reported to my grandmother, made him bear this treatment for many months. He was a crafty man, and resorted to many means to accomplish his purposes. Sometimes he had stormy, terrific ways, that made his victims tremble; sometimes he assumed a gentleness that he thought must surely subdue. Of the two, I preferred his stormy moods, although they left me trembling. He tried his utmost to corrupt the pure principles my grandmother had instilled. He peopled my young mind with unclean images, such as only a vile monster could think of. I turned from him with disgust and hatred. But he was my master. I was compelled to live under the same roof with him—where I saw a man forty years my senior daily violating the most sacred commandments of nature. He told me I was his property; that I must be subject to his will in all things. My soul revolted against the mean tyranny. But where could I turn for protection? No matter whether the slave girl be as black as ebony or as fair as her mistress. In either case, there is no shadow of law to protect her from insult, from violence, or even from death; all these are inflicted by fiends who bear the shape of men. The mistress, who ought to protect the helpless victim, has no other feelings towards her but those of jealousy and rage. The degradation, the wrongs, the vices, that grow out of slavery, are more than I can describe. They are greater than you would willingly believe. Surely, if you credited one half the truths that are told you concerning the helpless millions suffering in this cruel bondage, you at the north would not help to tighten the yoke. You surely would refuse to do for the master, on your own soil, the mean and cruel work which trained bloodhounds and the lowest class of whites do for him at the south.

Every where the years bring to all enough of sin and sorrow; but in slavery the very dawn of life is darkened by these shadows. Even the little child, who is accustomed to wait on her mistress and her children, will learn, before she is twelve years old, why it is that her mistress hates such and such a one among the slaves. Perhaps the child's own mother is among those hated ones. She listens to violent outbreaks of jealous passion, and cannot help understanding what is the cause. She will become prematurely knowing in evil things. Soon she will learn to tremble when she hears her master's footfall. She will be compelled to realize that she is no longer a child. If God has bestowed beauty upon her, it will prove her greatest curse. That which commands admiration in the white woman only hastens the degradation of the female slave. I know that some are too much brutalized by slavery to feel the humiliation of their position; but many slaves feel it most acutely, and shrink from the memory of it. I cannot tell how much I suffered in the presence of these wrongs, nor how I am still pained by the retrospect. My master met me at every turn, reminding me that I belonged to him, and swearing by heaven and earth that he would compel me to submit to him. If I went out for a breath of fresh air, after a day of unwearied toil, his footsteps dogged me. If I knelt by my mother's grave, his dark shadow fell on me even there. The light heart which nature had given me became heavy with sad forebodings. The other slaves in my master's house noticed the change. Many of them pitied me; but none dared to ask the cause. They had no need to inquire. They knew too well the guilty practices under that roof; and they were aware that to speak of them was an offence that never went unpunished.

Grandmother's Scorching Rebukes

I longed for some one to confide in. I would have given the world to have laid my head on my grandmother's faithful bosom, and told her all my troubles. But Dr. Flint swore he would kill me, if I was not as silent as the grave. Then, although my grandmother was all in all to me, I feared her as well as loved her. I had been accustomed to look up to her with a respect bordering upon awe. I was very young, and felt shamefaced about telling her such impure things, especially as I knew her to be very strict on such subjects. Moreover, she was a woman of a high spirit. She was usually very quiet in her demeanor; but if her indignation was once roused, it was not very easily quelled. I had been told that she once chased a white gentleman with a loaded pistol, because he insulted one of her daughters. I dreaded the consequences of a violent outbreak; and both pride and fear kept me silent. But though I did not confide in my grandmother, and even evaded her vigilant watchfulness and inquiry, her presence in the neighborhood was some protection to me. Though she had been a slave, Dr. Flint was afraid of her. He dreaded her scorching rebukes. Moreover, she was known and patronized by many people; and he did not wish to have his villainy made public. It was lucky for me that I did not live on a distant plantation, but in a town not so large that the inhabitants were ignorant of each other's affairs. Bad as are the laws and customs in a slaveholding community, the doctor, as a professional man, deemed it prudent to keep up some outward show of decency.

O, what days and nights of fear and sorrow that man caused me! Reader, it is not to awaken sympathy for myself that I am telling you truthfully what I suffered in slavery. I do it to kindle a flame of compassion in your hearts for my sisters who are still in bondage, suffering as I once suffered.

I once saw two beautiful children playing together. One was a fair white child; the other was her slave, and also her sister. When I saw them embracing each other, and heard their joyous laughter, I turned sadly away from the lovely sight. I foresaw the inevitable blight that would fall on the little slave's heart. I knew how soon her laughter would be changed to sighs. The fair child grew up to be a still fairer woman. From childhood to womanhood her pathway was blooming with flowers, and overarched by a sunny sky. Scarcely one day of her life had been clouded when the sun rose on her happy bridal morning.

How had those years dealt with her slave sister, the little playmate of her childhood? She, also, was very beautiful; but the flowers and sunshine of love were not for her. She drank the cup of sin, and shame, and misery, whereof her persecuted race are compelled to drink.

In view of these things, why are ye silent, ye free men and women of the north? Why do your tongues falter in maintenance of the right? Would that I had more ability! But my heart is so full, and my pen is so weak! There are noble men and women who plead for us, striving to help those who cannot help themselves. God bless them! God give them strength and courage to go on! God bless those, every where, who are laboring to advance the cause of humanity!

Mr. Flint's Character

I would ten thousand times rather that my children should be the half-starved paupers of Ireland than to be the most pampered among the slaves of America. I would rather drudge out my life on a cotton plantation, till the grave opened to give me rest, than to live with an unprincipled master and a jealous mistress. The felon's home in a penitentiary is preferable. He may repent, and turn from the error of his ways, and so find peace; but it is not so with a favorite slave. She is not allowed to have any pride of character. It is deemed a crime in her to wish to be virtuous.

Mrs. Flint possessed the key to her husband's character before I was born. She might have used this knowledge to counsel and to screen the young and the innocent among her slaves; but for them she had no sympathy. They were the objects of her constant suspicion and malevolence. She watched her husband with unceasing vigilance; but he was well practised in means to evade it. What he could not find opportunity to say in words he manifested in signs. He invented more than were ever thought of in a deaf and dumb asylum. I let them pass, as if I did not understand what he meant; and many were the curses and threats bestowed on me for my stupidity. One day he caught me teaching myself to write. He frowned, as if he was not well pleased; but I suppose he came to the conclusion that such an accomplishment might help to advance his favorite scheme. Before long, notes were often slipped into my hand. I would return them, saying, "I can't read them, sir." "Can't you?" he replied; "then I must read them to you." He always finished the reading by asking, "Do you understand?" Sometimes he would complain of the heat of the tea room, and order his supper to be placed on a small table in the piazza. He would seat himself there with a well-satisfied smile, and tell me to stand by and brush away the flies. He would eat very slowly, pausing between the mouthfuls. These intervals were employed in describing the happiness I was so foolishly throwing away, and in threatening me with the penalty that finally awaited my stubborn disobedience. He boasted much of the forbearance he had exercised towards me, and reminded me that there was a limit to his patience. When I succeeded in avoiding opportunities for him to talk to me at home, I was ordered to come to his office, to do some errand. When there, I was obliged to stand and listen to such language as he saw fit to address to me. Sometimes I so openly expressed my contempt for him that he would become violently enraged, and I wondered why he did not strike me. Circumstanced as he was, he probably thought it was better policy to be forbearing. But the state of things grew worse and worse daily. In desperation I told him that I must and would apply to my grandmother for protection. He threatened me with death, and worse than death, if I made any complaint to her. Strange to say, I did not despair. I was naturally of a buoyant disposition, and always I had a hope of somehow getting out of his clutches. Like many a poor, simple slave before me, I trusted that some threads of joy would yet be woven into my dark destiny.

Dr. Flint's Scheme

I had entered my sixteenth year, and every day it became more apparent that my presence was intolerable to Mrs. Flint. Angry words frequently passed between her and her husband. He had never punished me himself, and he would not allow any body else to punish me. In that respect, she was never satisfied; but, in her angry moods, no terms were too vile for her to bestow upon me. Yet I, whom she detested so bitterly, had far more pity for her than he had, whose duty it was to make her life happy. I never wronged her, or wished to wrong her; and one word of kindness from her would have brought me to her feet.

After repeated quarrels between the doctor and his wife, he announced his intention to take his youngest daughter, then four years old, to sleep in his apartment. It was necessary that a servant should sleep in the same room, to be on hand if the child stirred. I was selected for that office, and informed for what purpose that arrangement had been made. By managing to keep within sight of people, as much as possible, during the day time, I had hitherto succeeded in eluding my master, though a razor was often held to my throat to force me to change this line of policy. At night I slept by the side of my great aunt, where I felt safe. He was too prudent to come into her room. She was an old woman, and had been in the family many years. Moreover, as a married man, and a professional man, he deemed it necessary to save appearances in some degree. But he resolved to remove the obstacle in the way of his scheme; and he thought he had planned it so that he should evade suspicion. He was well aware how much I prized my refuge by the side of my old aunt, and he determined to dispossess me of it. The first night the doctor had the little child in his room alone. The next morning, I was ordered to take my station as nurse the following night. A kind Providence interposed in my favor. During the day Mrs. Flint heard of this new arrangement, and a storm followed. I rejoiced to hear it rage.

A Truthful Account

After a while my mistress sent for me to come to her room. Her first question was, "Did you know you were to sleep in the doctor's room?"

"Yes, ma'am."

"Who told you?"

"My master."

Will you answer truly all the questions I ask?"

"Yes, ma'am."

"Tell me, then, as you hope to be forgiven, are you innocent of what I have accused you?"

"I am."

She handed me a Bible, and said, "Lay your hand on your heart, kiss this holy book, and swear before God that you tell me the truth."

I took the oath she required, and I did it with a clear conscience.

"You have taken God's holy word to testify, your innocence," said she. "If you have deceived me, beware! Now take this stool, sit down, look me directly in the face, and tell me all that has passed between your master and you."

I did as she ordered. As I went on with my account her color changed frequently, she wept, and sometimes groaned. She spoke in tones so sad, that I was touched by her grief. The tears came to my eyes; but I was soon convinced that her emotions arose from anger and wounded pride. She felt that her marriage vows were desecrated, her dignity insulted; but she had no compassion for the poor victim of her husband's perfidy. She pitied herself as a martyr; but she was incapable of feeling for the condition of shame and misery in which her unfortunate, helpless slave was placed.

Yet perhaps she had some touch of feeling for me; for when the conference was ended, she spoke kindly, and promised to protect me. I should have been much comforted by this assurance if I could have had confidence in it; but my experiences in slavery had filled me with distrust. She was not a very refined woman, and had not much control over her passions. I was an object of her jealousy, and, consequently, of her hatred; and I knew I could not expect kindness or confidence from her under the circumstances in which I was placed. I could not blame her. Slaveholders' wives feel as other women would under similar circumstances. The fire of her temper kindled from small sparks, and now the flame became so intense that the doctor was obliged to give up his intended arrangement.

An Object of Care

I knew I had ignited the torch, and I expected to suffer for it afterwards; but I felt too thankful to my mistress for the timely aid she rendered me to care much about that. She now took me to sleep in a room adjoining her own. There I was an object of her especial care, though not of her especial comfort, for she spent many a sleepless night to watch over me. Sometimes I woke up, and found her bending over me. At other times she whispered in my ear, as though it was her husband who was speaking to me, and listened to hear what I would answer. If she startled me, on such occasions, she would glide stealthily away; and the next morning she would tell me I had been talking in my sleep, and ask who I was talking to. At last, I began to be fearful for my life. It had been often threatened; and you can imagine, better than I can describe, what an unpleasant sensation it must produce to wake up in the dead of night and find a jealous woman bending over you. Terrible as this experience was, I had fears that it would give place to one more terrible.

My mistress grew weary of her vigils; they did not prove satisfactory. She changed her tactics. She now tried the trick of accusing my master of crime, in my presence, and gave my name as the author of the accusation. To my utter astonishment, he replied, "I don't believe it; but if she did acknowledge it, you tortured her into exposing me." Tortured into exposing him! Truly, Satan had no difficulty in distinguishing the color of his soul! I understood his object in making this false representation. It was to show me that I gained nothing by seeking the protection of my mistress; that the power was still all in his own hands. I pitied Mrs. Flint. She was a second wife, many years the junior of her husband; and the hoary-headed miscreant was enough to try the patience of a wiser and better woman. She was completely foiled, and knew not how to proceed. She would gladly have had me flogged for my supposed false oath; but, as I have already stated, the doctor never allowed any one to whip me. The old sinner was politic. The application of the lash might have led to remarks that would have exposed him in the eyes of his children and grandchildren. How often did I rejoice that I lived in a town where all the inhabitants knew each other! If I had been on a remote plantation, or lost among the multitude of a crowded city, I should not be a living woman at this day.

The secrets of slavery are concealed like those of the Inquisition. My master was, to my knowledge, the father of eleven slaves. But did the mothers dare to tell who was the father of their children? Did the other slaves dare to allude to it, except in whispers among themselves? No, indeed! They knew too well the terrible consequences.

My grandmother could not avoid seeing things which excited her suspicions. She was uneasy about me, and tried various ways to buy me; but the never-changing answer was always repeated: "Linda does not belong to *me*. She is my daughter's property, and I have no legal right to sell her." The conscientious man! He was too scrupulous to *sell* me; but he had no scruples whatever about committing a much greater wrong against the helpless young girl placed under his guardianship, as his daughter's property. Sometimes my persecutor would ask me whether I would like to be sold. I told him I would rather be sold to any body than to lead such a life as I did. On such occasions he would assume the air of a very injured individual, and reproach me for my ingratitude. "Did I not take you into the house, and make you the companion of my own children?" he would say. "Have I ever treated you like a negro? I have never allowed you to be punished, not even to please your mistress. And this is the recompense I get, you ungrateful girl!" I answered that he had reasons of his own for screening me from punishment, and that the course he pursued made my mistress hate me and persecute me. If I wept, he would say, "Poor child! Don't cry! don't cry! I will make peace for you with your mistress. Only let me arrange matters in my own way. Poor, foolish girl! you don't know what is for your own good. I would cherish you. I would make a lady of you. Now go, and think of all I have promised you."

I did think of it.

Parental Relations

Reader, I draw no imaginary pictures of southern homes. I am telling you the plain truth. Yet when victims make their escape from this wild beast of Slavery, northerners consent to act the part of bloodhounds, and hunt the poor fugitive back into his den, "full of dead men's bones, and all uncleanness." Nay, more, they are not only willing, but proud, to give their daughters in marriage to slaveholders. The poor girls have romantic notions of a sunny clime, and of the flowering vines that all the year round shade a happy home. To what disappointments are they destined! The young wife soon learns that the husband in whose hands she has placed her happiness pays no regard to his marriage vows. Children of every shade of complexion play with her own fair babies, and too well she knows that they are born unto him of his own household. Jealousy and hatred enter the flowery home, and it is ravaged of its loveliness.

Southern women often marry a man knowing that he is the father of many little slaves. They do not trouble themselves about it. They regard such children as property, as marketable as the pigs on the plantation; and it is seldom that they do not make them aware of this by passing them into the slavetrader's hands as soon as possible, and thus getting them out of their sight. I am glad to say there are some honorable exceptions.

I have myself known two southern wives who exhorted their husbands to free those slaves towards whom they stood in a "parental relation;" and their request was granted. These husbands blushed before the superior nobleness of their wives' natures. Though they had only counselled them to do that which it was their duty to do, it commanded their respect, and rendered their conduct more exemplary. Concealment was at an end, and confidence took the place of distrust.

Though this bad institution deadens the moral sense, even in white women, to a fearful extent, it is not altogether extinct. I have heard southern ladies say of Mr. Such a one, "He not only thinks it no disgrace to be the father of those little niggers, but he is not ashamed to call himself their master. I declare, such things ought not to be tolerated in any decent society!"

The Sale of a Slave

William G. Eliot

The abuse of slaves did not end at the occasional whipping or mutilation for disobedience, running away, or a bad attitude. The casual buying, selling, trading, and abandonment of slaves proved an equally cruel treatment. All of these broke up married couples and separated slaves from their children, who were treated as casually as any other property and disposed of without any thought to the sentiment of their parents.

The sale of slaves often came about as a payment for debt or in the settlement of the estate of a deceased slaveowner. In addition, the slaveowners of the Chesapeake region and the northern tier of slave states found a profitable market for slaves in the cotton states of the Deep South, where in the early nineteenth century the market for raw cotton in the northern United States and England brought about high prices for plantation labor.

Nevertheless, many slaveowners held personal beliefs against breaking up slave families, and took the paternalistic view that the slaves' lives and well-being were their responsibility. One such family was that of a Reverend Delaney, who lived near Richmond, Virginia. Finding himself encumbered by debt, Reverend Delaney wrestled hard with the question of what to do with slaves he could no longer afford—and eventually decided the question against a man named Aleck, the most loyal and useful member of his household.

A bout twenty-five or thirty miles from Richmond, Virginia, in the year 1828, a family was living in the old-fashioned hospitable Virginia gentleman-farmer style, on a

From William G. Eliot, *The Story of Archer Alexander: From Slavery to Freedom* (Boston: Cupples, Upham, 1855).

place of some three hundred acres, which the young folks called Kalorama, because of the beautiful outlook from the old homestead, although the name was not used except in the immediate neighborhood.

The proprietor was a man of some consequence, the Rev. Mr. Delaney, who had been, before his marriage, in active discharge of his duties as a Presbyterian minister, but had retired from all except occasional services of special interest, although still familiarly called parson or doctor by his neighbors. His wife, who brought him the property, was a lady of great excellence, belonging to one of the best families of the State,—a warm-hearted, devout woman, a good manager, a faithful wife and mother. At the time of which I write, two sons and three daughters were growing up, the oldest of them eighteen years of age. There were ten or twelve families of slaves, numbering, in all, about seventy "head," old and young.

Upon one subject Mrs. Delaney was absolutely fixed. While believing that slavery was a divine institution, sanctioned by scripture from the time when "Cursed be Ham" was spoken, down to the return of the fugitive slave Onesimus by the apostle Paul,—subjects on which her husband had eloquently preached,—yet she felt deeply through her whole nature, as most of the well-born Southern women did, that there was a trust involved for which the slave owner was responsible to God almost as sacredly as for his own children. To all separation of families, therefore, except at their own choice or as a penalty for wrongdoing, she was firmly opposed. It had seldom occurred on the place, and she said it never should occur if she could help it. She had also succeeded in convincing, or at least in persuading, her husband to the same effect. But he wavered sometimes, under the pressure for money, and had even suggested the wisdom of selling off a few so as to better provide for the remainder.

Making Oneself Too Smart

Only once, however, had he distinctly overstepped the line, and that was a signal instance. It was in the case of a man named Aleck, a full black, forty-five years old, strong, stalwart, intelligent; in fact, his very best "hand." Somehow or other, this fellow had learned to read. Nobody knew how, but probably from the children and by chance opportunities. A good deal of discussion about slavery was going on at the time, which was not very far from the Missouri compromise days; and Aleck had got some advanced notions of which he was rather proud, talking them out rather freely among his fellows. In fact, "he made himself altogether too smart." At a colored prayer-meeting he had gone so far as to say that "by the 'Claration of 'Dependence all men was ekal," and that "to trade in men and women, jess like hogs and hosses, wasn't 'cordin' to gospel, nohow."

Of course, such talk as this would not do. It spread among the colored folk, and the white people began to hear of it. One of Mr. Delaney's neighbors came to see him about it, and after a while a committee of church-members called upon him with a formal expostulation. They urged upon him that his duty as a Christian man required that he should send Aleck South; "that it was not doing to his neighbors as he would be done by, to keep such a mischief-maker there; that a slave insurrection would be the next thing."

Mr. Delaney, being a good Christian, and believing in the divine authority for slavery, saw the justice of what was said. He knew that such notions as Aleck's were fanatical, and subversive of social order. "Servants, obey your masters," was good scripture; and he was Greek scholar enough to know that, in the original, "servant" meant bond-servant or slave. So he talked with Aleck and threatened him, but it did little good. Aleck kept at his work, but his mind was working too. He was getting spoilt for slavery. As Deacon Snodgrass emphatically said, "he was a demoralized nigger."

Still his kind mistress pleaded for him. "Don't sell him if you can help it. Chloe [Aleck's wife] will go distracted if you do; and her boy Archer, that his young master thinks so much of, will take it so hard!" Even she wavered, as her manner of pleading showed. She had begun to think of this sale as a necessity.

Money or Equivalent

Unfortunately, Mr. Delaney was in debt. He owed a good deal of money, for the farm had not been well managed. His neighbors said he was "too easy on his niggers," for that. A suit had gone against him for fifteen hundred dollars, on which judgment was given and execution issued. He went to Richmond to arrange it and Aleck drove him down, as he had often done before; for he was a fine-looking fellow and his master was proud of him. They stopped on Grace Street, at the house of his creditor, who came to the door, praised the horses and, with an eye to business, closely scrutinized the driver. When they went in and had pledged each other, according to the hospitable notions of the times, in stiff glasses of good old whiskey, Colonel Jones poured out a glassful and took it with his own hands to Aleck,—an unusual courtesy, at which the chattel was astonished; but it gave the colonel a good opportunity of satisfying himself that the man was sound in life and limb. "Well, Aleck," he said, "your master hasn't sold you yet. I've heard talk of it."—"No, *sir*," said he. "Massa ain't a-goin' to do it, nudder. He'd most as lib sell one of his own chilluns."—"All right," said the colonel, "you just hold on to that." Aleck showed his teeth, and looked greatly pleased.

As soon as the colonel went in, Mr. Delaney began to apologize for delays, and to ask for further time. But the colonel had made up his mind, and answered abruptly, "Now, I tell you what, parson (creditors with law on their side are apt to take liberties), there ain't no use in this kind of talk. Cash is the word. But I tell you how we *can* fix it, short metre. You just give me a bill of sale for that nigger Aleck out there, and it's done. He's a sassy boy and will get you into a big scrape some day; and you'd better get shet [rid] of him, anyway, for your own good and for the good of the country. There now, parson, the way I look at it, your religion and your pocket are on the same side. What do you say? But one thing's sure: money or its equiv-a-lent I'm a-going to have, down on the nail. There ain't no two ways about that."

Mr. Delaney hesitated and pleaded. He concluded to stay over night with his considerate friend. His duty seemed to him plain enough; but his feelings rebelled, and the thought of his wife increased the weakness. But he prayed over it at night, and again in the morning. His mind gradually cleared up, especially when, after breakfast, the accounts were laid before him and the necessity of speedy action became plain.

"What are you going to do with Aleck?" he asked, unconsciously betraying that the decision was already made. "Why, now," answered the colonel with an emphatic gesture, "that's just where it is. There's a kind of prov-i-dence in it. Here's my neighbor, Jim Buckner, that's making up a gang to go South, and he wants a fancy nigger for a customer in Charleston, and he knows Aleck and told me to get him and he'd pay judgment *and* costs. It's an awful big price, but he's as rich as creases [Croesus] and don't care. Such a chance wouldn't never happen again in a lifetime, and Aleck would have a first-rate master besides. But he'll have to hold his impudent jaw down there, *I tell you.*"

It came hard, but the bill of sale was signed, and the debt paid. Every thing was done as Colonel Jones said; "quiet and civil, and without fuss. What's the use of hurting the boy's feelings, and your'n too, when it's got to be done?" So Aleck was sent on a pretended errand to a place near the slave-jail, taken quietly by Jim Buckner and his men, handcuffed, carried South the same evening, and *nobody at Kalorama ever heard of him again.* It was his death and burial.

The Order of Providence

The next day Mr. Delaney returned home, arriving late in the evening. Great was the excitement when it was known that Aleck had been sold South "to pay massa's debts," and had gone off with Buckner's gang. Poor Chloe, his wife, was dumfounded. She sat down, rocked her body backward and forward, and groaned aloud, "O Lord God, oh, dear Jesus, what has ole massa gone and done! O Lord Jesus, whar was you when he done it!" But there was no help for it, no hope for her. The next day's work must go on: so she cooked and washed as usual, heavy-hearted but silent.

"You see how it is," said Deacon Snodgrass; "these niggers don't have no feelings like white folks. Anyhow, it's only as if her old man had died. The thing happens every day, and has got to happen. It's the order of Prov-i-dence."

Mrs. Delaney was deeply grieved. The young master, Thomas, took it hardest at first, and said right out, "it was a damned shame." But his father rebuked his profanity, and explained the case to him as one of unavoidable Christian duty. Aleck's son Archer was too young to understand it; but he kept close to his mother, who, after that, never liked to lose sight of him. The neighbors generally said it was a good thing; "that Delaney's niggers had got too uppish, and would now be brought down a peg. It was high time for an example."

Some slaveowners tried to keep slave families together.

Two years had already passed since that "taking down a peg" had occurred; but, on the whole, things had not improved. The farm kept deteriorating in value, worn out by exhausting crops of corn and tobacco. One of the hands ran away and escaped. Another who tried it, with his wife and child, was caught and brought back; but they had suffered so much from exposure and in the struggle with their captors, who *had an unmanageable dog with them,* that they were never of much account afterwards. From such experience the rest could not fail to learn the wisdom of submission and contentment. Yet a spirit of uneasiness prevailed, so unreasoning is the African mind. The increasing probability of being sold South, and the difficulty of running away, did not seem to have a soothing influence.

Settling an Estate

In 1831 Mr. Delaney died suddenly, leaving no will and many debts. The estate was administered upon, and about one-half the land, with three or four families of slaves, were sold to pay the pressing debts. The rest of the property was divided, under the law, among the widow and children. In this division Chloe fell to the widow's share; her boy Archer, now eighteen years old, to the "young master," Mrs. Delaney's oldest son. But Chloe, Aleck's "widow," had run down very sadly. It really seemed almost as if she had had feelings like white people, and Aleck's being sold South was in some way or other very different to her from a divine dispensation of bereavement. A clergyman talked with her; but when he said, "The Lord gave, and the Lord hath taken away; blessed be the name of the Lord,"—she said with sobs, "O Lord, massa! please don't talk dat way! I can't see it, nohow!" She was no longer cheerful and full of jokes, but stolid and heavy-hearted, taking no interest in any thing except her boy Archie. It was not long before she had to lose him too, though not by death.

Mrs. Delaney's oldest son, Thomas, whom Chloe had nursed in his infancy, made up his mind to emigrate to Missouri, the new land of promise in the West. His mother and the rest of the family would stay in the old place. He quietly made all his arrangements, sent part of his valuables forward to Guyandotte to wait for him there, and when quite ready, one day after dinner, told Archer, his foster-brother, to saddle up the horses and get ready for a start, so as to make twenty miles before night set in.

Of course, the old tradition of not separating families had been broken up, in the settlement of the estate. The law is no respecter of persons or feelings. It allows little place for sentiment, and the family plate is worth the silver in it; no more. Everything had been appraised at its value, slaves included; and, if families could not be kept together, it was nobody's fault. They were sold under the hammer, "to the best advantage."

It is a great mistake to suppose that the chief hardships of slavery consisted in acts of severity or cruelty. Such did frequently occur, for irresponsible power over an inferior race is sure to result in its abuse; but they were the comparatively rare exceptions, and in no part of the South were they the rule. The vast majority of slave owners ameliorated the condition of slavery; that is, so far as they conveniently could, consistently with their own interests, the maintenance of subordination, and a friendly regard to the rights of their neighbors. They looked carefully after the comfort of their "families" up to a certain point, treated them with humanity and sometimes with indulgence and tenderness. Nevertheless they were "chattels" (Anglice, "cattle"),—in the eye of the law, property subject to seizure and sale. The exigencies of debt, so common in the unthrifty Southern management; the death of the owner, and consequent necessity of dividing the estate; the commission of faults of impudence or petty criminality, to say nothing of the whims and caprices of the master or mistress,—all were common and lawful causes of trouble. Over the best and most pampered slave the sword of uncertainty always hung, suspended by an invisible hair; from which it came to pass, that, under the best of circumstances, the best condition of slavery was worse than the worst condition of freedom. The blacks are a docile and easily controlled race. Subordination does not come hard to them. But at this moment,—twenty years after they have had the trial of freedom, trammelled as it has been by not a few hardships and social oppressions, and by greater cruelties in some sections than slavery itself witnessed,—I doubt if a man or woman could be found who would exchange freedom, such as it is, for the old relation under the best master that ever lived.

Punishment

Charles Ball

> Charles Ball was born a slave in Maryland, the grandson of
> an African sold in Calvert County, Maryland. Ball was
> forcibly separated from his mother as a child and, when his
> first owner died, he was sold to another Maryland family.
> Eventually he fell into the hands of a slave trader who, seek-
> ing more profitable markets for his property in the South,
> marched Ball as far as the Carolinas. Later, Ball would twice
> escape from his bondage and eventually publish two popular
> books detailing his experiences as a slave in the South.
>
> In an early chapter of his 1859 book *Fifty Years in Chains,*
> Ball details his first days with a new master in South Car-
> olina. He witnesses a group of slaves at work in a cotton field,
> where he falls into conversation with a slave foreman. Notic-
> ing that the old gentleman wears a peculiar piece of clothing,
> the curious Ball asks for a history—and then hears a horrific
> tale of cruelty.

The man who was foreman of the field, was a person of
good sense for the condition of life in which fortune
had placed him, and spoke to me freely of his hard lot. I observed that under his shirt, which was very ragged, he wore
a piece of fine linen cloth, apparently part of an old shirt,
wrapped closely round his back, and confined in front by
strings, tied down his breast. I asked him why he wore that
piece of gentleman's linen under his shirt, and shall give his
reply in his own words as well as I can recollect them, at a
distance of near thirty years.

From Charles Ball, *Fifty Years in Chains; or, The Life of an American Slave* (New York:
H. Dayton, 1859).

"I have always been a hard working man, and have suffered a great deal from hunger in my time. It is not possible for a man to work hard every day for several months, and get nothing but a peck [one-quarter bushel] of corn a week to eat, and not feel hungry. When a man is hungry, you know (if you have ever been hungry), he must eat whatever he can get. I have not tasted meat since last Christmas, and we have had to work uncommonly hard this summer. Master has a flock of sheep, that run in the woods, and they come every night to sleep in the lane near the house. Two weeks ago last Saturday, when we quit work at night, I was very hungry, and as we went to the house we passed along the lane where the sheep lay. There were nearly fifty of them, and some were very fat. The temptation was more than I could bear. I caught one of them, cut its head off with the hoe that I carried on my shoulder, and threw it under the fence. About midnight, when all was still about the house, I went out with a knife, took the sheep into the woods, and dressed it by the light of the moon. The carcass I took home, and after cutting it up, placed it in the great kettle over a good fire, intending to boil it and divide it, when cooked, between my fellow-slaves (whom I knew to be as hungry as I was) and myself.

Caught in the Act

Unfortunately for me, master Tom, who had been out amongst his friends that day, had not returned at bedtime; and about one o'clock in the morning, at the time when I had a blazing fire under the kettle, I heard the sound of the feet of a horse coming along the lane. The kitchen walls were open so that the light of my fire could not be concealed, and in a moment I heard the horse blowing at the front of the house. Conscious of my danger, I stripped my shirt from my back, and pushed it into the boiling kettle, so as wholly to conceal the flesh of the sheep. I had scarcely completed this act of precaution, when master Tom burst into the kitchen, and with a terrible oath, asked me what I was doing so late at night, with a great fire in the kitchen. I replied, 'I am going to wash my shirt, master, and am boiling it to get it clean.' 'Washing your shirt at this time of night!' said he, 'I will let you know that you are not to sit up all night and be lazy and good for nothing all day. There shall be no boiling of shirts here on Sunday morning.' and thrusting his cane into the kettle, he raised my shirt out and threw it on the kitchen floor.

"He did not at first observe the mutton, which rose to the surface of the water as soon as the shirt was removed; but, after giving the shirt a kick towards the door, he again turned his face to the fire, and seeing a leg standing several inches out of the pot, he demanded of me what I had in there and where I had got this meat! Finding that I was detected, and that the whole matter must be discovered, I said,—'Master, I am hungry, and am cooking my supper.' 'What is it you have in here?' 'A sheep,' said I, and as the words were uttered, he knocked me down with his cane, and after beating me severely, ordered me to cross my hands until he bound me fast with a rope that hung in the kitchen, and answered the double purpose of a clothes line and a cord to tie us with when we were to be whipped. He put out the fire under the kettle, drew me into the yard, tied me fast to the mill-post, and leaving me there for the night, went and called one of the negro boys to put his horse in the stable, and went to his bed. The cord was bound so tightly round my wrists, that before morning the blood had burst out under my finger nails; but I suppose my master slept soundly for all that.

I was afraid to call any one to come and release me from my torment, lest a still more terrible punishment might overtake me.

Oaths and Imprecations

"I was permitted to remain in this situation until long after sunrise the next morning, which being Sunday, was quiet and still; my fellow-slaves being permitted to take their rest after the severe toil of the past week, and my old master and the two young ones having no occasion to rise to call the hands to the field, did not think of interrupting their morning slumbers, to release me from my painful confinement. However, when the sun was risen about an hour, I heard the noise of persons moving in the great house, and soon after a loud and boisterous conversation, which I well knew portended no good to me. At length they all three came into the yard where I lay lashed to the post, and approaching me, my old master asked me if I had any accomplices in stealing the sheep. I told them none—that it was entirely my own act— and that none of my fellow-slaves had any hand in it. This was the truth; but if any of my companions had been concerned with me, I should not have betrayed them; for such an act of treachery could not have alleviated the dreadful punishment which I knew awaited me, and would only have involved them in the same misery.

"They called me a thief, loaded me with oaths and imprecations, and each one proposed the punishment which he deemed the most appropriate to the enormity of the crime that I had committed. Master Tom was of opinion, that I should be lashed to the post at the foot of which I lay, and that each of my fellow-slaves should be compelled to give me a dozen lashes in turn, with a roasted and greased hickory *gad* [prod], until I had received, in the whole, two hundred and fifty lashes on my bare back, and that he would stand by, with the whip in his hand, and *compel* them not to spare me; but after a short debate this was given up, as it would probably render me unable to work in the field again for several weeks. My master Ned was in favor of giving me a dozen lashes every morning for a month, with the whip; but my old master said, this would be attended with too much trouble, and besides, it would keep me from my work, at least half an hour every morning, and proposed, in his turn, that I should not be whipped at all, but that the carcass of the sheep should be taken from the kettle in its half-boiled condition, and hung up in the kitchen loft without salt; and that I should be compelled to subsist on this putrid mutton without any other food, until it should be consumed. This suggestion met the approbation of my young masters, and would have been adopted, had not mistress at this moment come into the yard, and hearing the intended punishment, loudly objected to it, because the mutton would, in a day or two, create such an offensive stench, that she and my young mistresses would not be able to remain in the house. My mistress swore dreadfully, and cursed me for an ungrateful sheep thief, who, after all her kindness in giving me soup and warm bread when I was sick last winter, was always stealing every thing I could get hold of. She then said to my master, that such villainy ought not to be passed over in a slight manner, and that as crimes, such as this, concerned the whole country, my punishment ought to be public for the purpose of example; and advised him to have me whipped that same afternoon, at five o'clock; first giving notice to the neighborhood to come and see the spectacle, and to bring with them their slaves, that they might be witnesses to the consequences of stealing sheep.

Cruel Mistresses

"They then returned to the house to breakfast; but as the pain in my hands and arms produced by the ligatures of the cord with which I was bound, was greater than I could bear, I now felt exceedingly sick, and lost all knowledge of my situation. They told me I fainted; and when I recovered my faculties, I found myself lying in the shade of the house, with my hands free, and all the white persons in my master's family standing around me. As soon as I was able to stand, the rope was tied round my neck, and the other end again fastened to the mill post. My mistress said I had only pretended to faint; and master Tom said, I would have something worth fainting for before night. He was faithful to his promise; but, for the present, I was suffered to sit on the grass in the shade of the house.

"As soon as breakfast was over, my two young masters had their horses saddled, and set out to give notice to their friends of what had happened, and to invite them to come and see me punished for the crime I had committed. My mistress gave me no breakfast, and when I begged one of the black boys whom I saw looking at me through the pales, to bring me some water in a gourd to drink, she ordered him to bring it from a puddle in the lane. My mistress has always been very cruel to all her black people.

"I remained in this situation until about eleven o'clock, when one of my young mistresses came to me and gave me a piece of johnny-cake [cornbread] about the size of my hand, perhaps larger than my hand, telling me at the same time, that my fellow-slaves had been permitted to re-boil the mutton that I had left in the kettle, and make their breakfast of it, but that her mother would not allow her to give me any part of it. It was well for them that I had parboiled it with my shirt, and so defiled it that it was unfit for the table of my master, otherwise, no portion of it would have fallen to the black people—as it was, they had as much meat as they could consume in two days, for which I had to suffer.

The Witnesses Gather

"About twelve o'clock, one of my young masters returned, and soon afterwards the other came home. I heard them tell my old master that they had been round to give notice of my offence to the neighboring planters, and that several of them would attend to see me flogged, and would bring with them some of their slaves, who might be able to report to their companions what had been done to me for stealing.

"It was late in the afternoon before any of the gentlemen came; but, before five o'clock, there were more than twenty white people, and at least fifty black ones present, the latter of whom had been compelled, by their masters, to come and see me punished. Amongst others, an overseer from a neighboring estate attended; and to him was awarded the office of executioner. I was stripped of my shirt, and the waistband of my trousers was drawn closely round me, below my hips, so as to expose the whole of my back, in its entire length.

"It seems that it had been determined to beat me with thongs of raw cow-hide, for the overseer had two of these in his hands, each about four feet long; but one of the gentlemen present said this might bruise my back so badly, that I could not work for some time; perhaps not for a week or two; and as I could not be spared from the field without disadvantage to my master's crop, he suggested a different plan, by which, in his opinion, the greatest degree of pain could be inflicted on me, with the least danger of rendering me unable to work. As he was a large planter, and had more than fifty slaves, all were disposed to be guided by his counsels, and my master said he would submit the matter entirely to him as a man of judgment and experience in such cases. He then desired my master to have a dozen pods of red pepper boiled in half a gallon of water, and desired the overseer to lay aside his thongs of raw-hide, and put a new cracker of silk, to the lash of his negro whip. Whilst these preparations were being made, each of my thumbs were lashed closely to the end of a stick about three feet long, and a chair being placed beside the mill post, I was compelled to raise my hands and place the stick, to which my thumbs were bound, over the top of the post, which is about eighteen inches square; the chair was then taken from under me,

Slavery in the Low Country

The conditions of slavery varied from region to region in the South. The reasons were economic: In general, certain crops could be efficiently produced only on large estates, and such estates could most efficiently be worked by large numbers of slaves. Historian Peter Kolchin, in his work American Slavery, 1619–1877, *describes how this phenomenon made the low country of South Carolina and Georgia the most slave-intensive region of the United States.*

At the opposite extreme was the low country of South Carolina (and, after the middle of the eighteenth century, Georgia), the area of the American mainland where slaveholding patterns most closely approached (without, however, reaching) those of the Caribbean. Because rice planters had to invest in complex irrigation systems needed alternately to flood and drain the land, rice, like sugar, was most and I was left hanging by the thumbs, with my face towards the post, and my feet about a foot from the ground. My two great toes were then tied together, and drawn down the post as far as my joints could be stretched; the cord was passed round the post two or three times and securely fastened. In this posture I had no power of motion, except in my neck, and could only move that at the expense of beating my face against the side of the post.

Pleading in Vain

"The pepper tea was now brought, and poured into a basin to cool, and the overseer was desired to give me a dozen lashes just above the waist-band; and not to cover a space of more than four inches on my back, from the waist-band upwards. He obeyed the injunction faithfully, but slowly, and each crack of the whip was followed by a sensation as painful as if a red hot iron had been drawn across my back. When the twelve strokes had been given, the operation was

---

efficiently cultivated on a large scale. Spurred by cultivation of rice—and, at the end of the eighteenth century, Sea Island cotton—slavery was more pervasive and slaveholdings were on the average much larger in the low country than anywhere else in America. As early at 1726, only a generation after the beginning of substantial rice cultivation, slaves made up more than 70 percent of the population in South Carolina's St. George Parish, and two-thirds of those slaves lived on holdings of more than 25. By the end of the eighteenth century, slaveholding was much more concentrated, with slaves composing about 84 percent of the low country's rural population and holdings with hundreds of slaves common; in 1790, the 11 parishes that made up the Charleston District contained 79 holdings with 100 or more slaves. Absenteeism was common among wealthy planters, many of whom preferred to spend their time in increasingly elegant Charleston rather than among "brutish" Africans on their isolated estates.

suspended, and a black man, one of the slaves present, was compelled to wash the gashes in my skin, with the scalding pepper tea, which was yet so hot that he could not hold his hand in it. This doubly-burning liquid was thrown into my raw and bleeding wounds, and produced a tormenting smart, beyond the description of language. After a delay of ten minutes, by the watch, I received another dozen lashes, on the part of my back which was immediately above the bleeding and burning gashes of the former whipping; and again the biting, stinging, pepper tea was applied to my lacerated and trembling muscles. This operation was continued at regular intervals, until I had received ninety-six lashes, and my back was cut and scalded from end to end. Every stroke of the whip had drawn blood; many of the gashes were three inches long; my back burned as if it had been covered by a coat of hot embers, mixed with living coals; and I felt my flesh quiver like that of animals that have been slaughtered by the butcher and are flayed whilst yet half alive. My face was bruised, and my nose bled profusely, for in the madness of my agony, I had not been able to refrain from beating my head violently against the post.

"Vainly did I beg and implore for mercy. I was kept bound to the post with my whole weight hanging upon my thumbs, an hour and a half, but it appeared to me that I had entered upon eternity, and that my sufferings would never end. At length, however, my feet were unbound, and afterwards my hands; but when released from the cords, I was so far exhausted as not to be able to stand, and my thumbs were stiff and motionless. I was carried into the kitchen, and laid on a blanket, where my mistress came to see me; and after looking at my lacerated back, and telling me that my wounds were only skin deep, said I had come off well, after what I had done, and that I ought to be thankful that it was not worse with me. She then bade me not to groan so loud, nor make so much noise, and left me to myself. I lay in this condition until it was quite dark, by which time the burning of my back had much abated, and was succeeded by an aching soreness, which rendered me unable to turn over, or bend my spine in the slightest manner. My mistress again visited me, and brought with her about half a pound of fat bacon, which she made one of the black women roast before the fire on a fork, until the oil ran freely from it, and then rub it warm over my back. This was repeated until I was greased from the neck to the hips, effectually. An old blanket was then thrown over me, and I was left to pass the night alone. Such was the terror stricken into my fellow-slaves, by the example made of me, that although they loved and pitied me, not one of them dared to approach me during this night.

A Return to Work

"My strength was gone, and I at length fell asleep, from which I did not awake until the horn was blown the next morning, to call the people to the corn crib, to receive their weekly allowance of a peck of corn. I did not rise, nor attempt to join the other people, and shortly afterwards my master entered the kitchen, and in a soft and gentle tone of voice, asked me if I was dead. I answered him that I was not dead, and making some effort, found I was able to get upon my feet. My master had become frightened when he missed me at the corn crib, and being suddenly seized with an apprehension that I was dead, his heart had become softened, not with compassion for my sufferings, but with the fear of losing his best field hand; but when he saw me stand before him erect, and upright, the recollection of the lost sheep revived in his mind, and with it, all his feelings of revenge against the author of its death.

"'So you are not dead yet, you thieving rascal,' said he, and cursing me with many bitter oaths, ordered me to go along to the crib and get my corn, and go to work with the rest of the hands. I was forced to obey, and taking my basket of corn from the door of the crib, placed it in the kitchen loft, and went to the field with the other people.

"Weak and exhausted as I was, I was compelled to do the work of an able hand, but was not permitted to taste the mutton, which was all given to the others, who were carefully guarded whilst they were eating, lest they should give me some of it."

This man's back was not yet well. Many of the gashes made by the lash were yet sore, and those that were healed had left long white stripes across his body. He had no notion of leaving the service of his tyrannical master, and his spirit was so broken and subdued that he was ready to suffer and to bear all his hardships: not, indeed, without complaining, but without attempting to resist his oppressors or to escape from their power. I saw him often whilst I remained at this place, and ventured to tell him once, that if I had a master who would abuse me as he had abused him, I would run away. "Where could I run, or in what place could I conceal myself?" said he. "I have known many slaves who ran away, but they were always caught and treated worse afterwards than they had been before. I have heard that there is a place called Philadelphia, where the black people are all free, but I do not know which way it lies, nor what road I should take to go there; and if I knew the way, how could I hope to get there? would not the patrol be sure to catch me?"

I pitied this unfortunate creature, and was at the same time fearful that, in a short time, I should be equally the object of pity myself. How well my fears were justified.

Chapter 4

Defiance, Rebellion, and Escape

Chapter Preface

For their North American owners, African slaves presented two crucial advantages over other forms of labor: They could be held for life, and they had almost no hope of escape. Many factors worked against would-be runaways and rebels among the slave population. First, they lived in a completely foreign country, and in most places, they were a long way from any possible assistance from sympathetic fellow slaves or abolitionists. Second, they could easily be betrayed by fellow slaves in whom they placed their confidence. Bounties and rewards for runaway slaves were always widely advertised in newspapers, by word of mouth, and on posters. Anyone laying plans for escape had to face the fact that capture was almost certain and also meant a harsh punishment when the owner whipped, branded, and tortured the runaway to set a frightening example for those who had remained behind.

Nevertheless, there were rebellions and resistance among the slaves of North America. A 1739 rebellion in South Carolina killed several white inhabitants of that colony. Gabriel Prosser (in Virginia) and Denmark Vesey (in South Carolina) both made elaborate plans for slave revolts before being betrayed and discovered. An African American visionary named Nat Turner led a roving band of black marauders through Southampton County, Virginia, in 1831. The Turner Rebellion brought the deaths of fifty-nine whites before being put down, and Turner himself managed to elude capture for another six weeks.

A more common form of rebellion was the escape of the individual slave to a free country such as Canada. Runaways became more common as the nineteenth century progressed, taking advantage of the growing abolitionist sentiment in the North and the system of safe houses known as the Underground Railroad. Hundreds of slaves were personally escorted out of bondage by abolitionists disguised as slave owners.

During the Civil War, slave resistance grew more widespread. When masters went away to war, slaves left behind often refused to work, attacked their overseers, or slipped away from their slave quarters permanently. African Americans in slavery also took every possible chance, especially when the Northern armies drew near, to run for freedom.

Finding Strength in Religion

James L. Smith

> Born in the Northern Neck of Virginia, James L. Smith experienced all the terrors of slavery, despite the fact that he managed to carve out some independence from his master. As he grew older, he realized that his fellow slaves had many other ways of striking out on their own, one of the most effective being conversion to the Christian religion. In their own church, and during their own prayer meetings, slaves could give full expression to their sorrows, fears, and yearnings. Smith found his own conversion to be the most powerful experience of his life, one that fortified him against a hard life and the unjust treatment of his owners.

I ran the shop for one year, during which time my young master became jealous of me. He thought I was making more money for myself than for him; it was not so, he was mistaken about it. What little I did earn for myself was justly my own. While I was away enjoying myself one Christmas day, he took an ox-cart with my brother, for Heathsville. The driving devolved on my brother. My master carried off my tools and every thing that was in the shop; he hired me out to a man who was considered by every one to be the worst one in Heathsville, whose name was Mr. Lacky, advising him "to keep me very strict, for I was knowing most too much." I lived with him three years. and managed so as to escape the cowhide all the time I was there, saving

From *Autobiography of James L. Smith, Including, Also, Reminiscences of Slave Life, Recollections of the War, Education of Freedmen, Causes of the Exodus, Etc.* (Norwich, CT: Press of the Bulletin Co., 1881).

once. I strove by my prudence and correctness of demeanor to avoid exciting his evil passions. While learning the shoe-maker's trade, I was about eighteen years old. At this time I became deeply interested in my soul's salvation; the white people held a prayer meeting in Fairfield one evening in a private house; I attended the meeting that evening, but was not permitted to go in the same room, but only allowed to go in an adjoining room. While there I found peace in believing, and in this happy state of mind I went home rejoicing and praising the Lord for what he had done for me. A few Sabbath's following, I united with the Church in Fairfield. Soon after I was converted I commenced holding meetings among the people, and it was not long before my fame began to spread as an exhorter. I was very zealous, so much so that I used to hold meetings all night, especially if there were any concerned about their immortal soul.

Twenty-Four Miles in a Day

I remember in one instance that having quit work about sundown on a Saturday evening, I prepared to go ten miles to hold a prayer meeting at Sister Gould's. Quite a number assembled in the little cabin, and we continued to sing and pray till daybreak, when it broke. All went to their homes, and I got about an hour's rest while Sister Gould was preparing breakfast. Having partaken of the meal, she, her daughter and myself set out to hold another meeting two miles further; this lasted till about five o'clock, when we returned. Then I had to walk back ten miles to my home, making in all twenty-four miles that day. How I ever did it, lame as I was, I cannot tell, but I was so zealous in the work that I did not mind going any distance to attend a prayer meeting. I actually walked a greater part of the distance fast asleep; I knew the road pretty well. There used to be a great many run-aways in that section, and they would hide away in the woods and swamps, and if they found a person alone as I was, they would spring out at them and rob them. As this thought came into my head during my lonely walk, thinks I, it won't do for me to go to sleep, and I began to look about me for some weapon of defence; I took my jack-knife from my pocket and opened it; now I am ready to stab the first one that tackles me, I said; but try as I would, I commenced to nod, nod, till I was fast asleep again. The long walk and the exertion of carrying on the meeting had nearly used me up.

The way in which we worshiped is almost indescribable. The singing was accompanied by a certain ecstasy of motion, clapping of hands, tossing of heads, which would continue without cessation about half an hour; one would lead off in a kind of recitative style, others joining in the chorus. The old house partook of the ecstasy; it rang with their jubilant shouts, and shook in all its joints. It is not to be wondered at that I fell asleep, for when I awoke I found I had lost my knife, and the fact that I would now have to depend on my own muscle, kept me awake till I had reached the neighborhood of my home. There was a lane about half a mile from the house, on each side of which was a ditch to drain the road, and was nearly half full of water; as I neared this lane I fell asleep again, as the first thing I knew I was in the ditch; I had walked right off into it, best clothes and all. Such a paddling to get out you never saw. I was wide awake enough now you may rest assured, and went into the house sick enough; my feet were all swollen, and I was laid up for two or three days. My mistress came in to see me, and said I must have medicine. I had to bear it, and she dosed me well.

Who Is Master?

As soon as I was able, I went to work. I had a shop all to myself. My master lived five miles away, but would come once a week and take all the earnings; some weeks I would make a great deal, then I would keep some back for myself, as I had worked for it. In this way I saved at one time fifteen dollars; I went to the store, bought a piece of cloth, carried it to the tailor and had a suit made—I had already bought a watch, and had a chain and seal. You can imagine how I looked the following Sunday; I was very proud and loved to dress well, and all the young people used to make a great time over me; it was Brother Payne here, and Brother Payne there; in fact, I was nearly everywhere.

The other slaves were obliged to be on the plantation when the horn blew, at daybreak, but sometimes I did not get home till twelve o'clock; sometimes it would be night, and I always escaped a whipping. The first Sunday that I was arrayed in my new suit, I was passing the court house bounds, when I saw my master and a man named Betts standing near by. Betts caught sight of me; says he: "Lindsey, come here." Not knowing what he wanted, I went to him; whereupon he commenced looking first at me, then at my master; then at my master, then at me; finally he said: "Who is master; Lindsey or you, for he dresses better than you do? Does he own you, or do you own him?"

From a child I had always felt that I wanted to be free. I could not bear the thought of belonging to any one, and so when I ran away, my mind was made up all in a sudden. My master came as far as Philadelphia to look for me; and, my brother says, when he came back without me, he became a very demon on the plantation, cutting and slashing, cursing and swearing at the slaves till there was no living with him. He seemed to be out of his head; and for hours would set looking straight into the fire; when spoken to, he would say: "I can't think what made Lindsey leave me."

One day he ordered my brother and a man named Daniel to move the barn from where it set further out to one side. So my brother went to work, with two or three others, and had raised it about three or four feet, when something gave way; and, as they were under the barn, they all ran out. My master seeing this became furious. "How dare you to run? You shall stay under there, if you get crushed to pieces!" So saying, he went into the house and got the rawhide. "Now," says he, "the first one who runs, I'll cut to pieces." He then took his place inside the barn, and commanded them to go on with their work, while he looked on.

They began to turn the screw, when some timber from above fell right across the door, completely blockading it.

Master was shut up in the barn, and it was impossible for him to get out. Why he did not jump out, when the creaking sound gave him warning, no one can tell; he seemed to sit back there, in a dazed sort of a way. There was a rush to rescue him, and he was found all mangled and bruised, with the rawhide grasped tightly in his hand. My brother says he only gasped once or twice after he was brought out.

Stealing Away to Meetings

When Nat Turner's insurrection broke out [in 1831], the colored people were forbidden to hold meetings among themselves. Nat Turner was one of the slaves who had quite a large army; he was the captain to free his race. Notwithstanding our difficulties, we used to steal away to some of the quarters to have our meetings. One Sabbath I went on a plantation about five miles off, where a slave woman had lost a child the day before, and as it was to be buried that day, we went to the "great house" to get permission from the master if we could have the funeral then. He sent back word for us to bury the child without any funeral services. The child was deposited in the ground, and that night we went off nearly a mile to a lonely cabin on Griffin Furshee's plantation, where we assembled about fifty or seventy of us in number; we were so happy that we had to give vent to the feelings of our hearts, and were making more noise than we realized. The master, whose name was Griffin Furshee, had gone to bed, and being awakened by the noise, took his cane and his servant boy and came where the sound directed him. While I was exhorting, all at once the door opened and behold there he stood, with his white face looking in upon us. As soon as I saw the face I stopped suddenly, without even waiting to say amen.

The people were very much frightened; with throbbing hearts some of them went up the log chimney, others broke out through the back door, while a few, who were more self-composed, stood their ground.

When the master came in, he wanted to know what we were doing there, and asked me if I knew that it was against the law for niggers to hold meetings. I expected every moment that he would fly at me with his cane; he did not, but only threatened to report me to my master. He soon left us to ourselves, and this was the last time he disturbed us in our meetings. His object in interrupting us was to find out whether we were plotting some scheme to raise an insurrection among the people. Before this, the white people held a quarterly meeting in the Fairfield Church, commencing Saturday, and continuing eight days and nights without cessation.

A Change of Heart

The religious excitement that existed at that time was so great that the people did not leave the church for their meals, but had them brought to them. There were many souls converted. The colored people attended every night. The white people occupied the part next to the altar, while the colored people took the part assigned them next to the door, where they held a protracted meeting among them-

A soul is converted in church as others look on.

selves. Sometimes, while we were praying, the white people would be singing, and when we were singing they would be praying; each gave full vent to their feelings, yet there was no discord or interruption with the two services. On Wednesday night, the fourth day from the commencement of the meeting, a colored woman by the name of Nancy Merrill, was converted, and when she experienced a change of heart she shouted aloud, rejoicing in the richness of her new found hope. Thursday night, the next evening, the meeting still continued.

By this time the excitement was on the increase among both parties, and it bid fair to hold eight days longer; but right in the midst of the excitement some one came to the door of the church and nodded to the sexton to come to the door; as soon as he did go to the door some one there told him to speak to Nancy Merrill, the new convert, and tell her to come to the door, for he wanted to speak to her. She went, and, behold it was a slave trader, who had bought her during the day from her mistress! As soon as she went to the door, he seized and bound her, and then took her off to her cabin home to get her two boys he had bought also. The sexton came back and reported to us what had taken place.

This thrilling and shocking news sent a sharp shiver through every heart; it went through the church like wild-fire; it broke up the meeting entirely among both parties; in less than half an hour every one left the church for home. This woman had a daughter in Fairfield, where I learned my trade, and I hastened home, as soon as possible, to tell the girl what had happened to her mother. She was standing by the fire in the kitchen as I entered—she was the servant girl of John Langsdon, the man who taught me the shoemaker's trade. As soon as I related to her this sad news she fell to the floor as though she had been shot by a pistol; and, as soon as she had recovered a little from the shock we started for her mother's cabin home, reaching there just in time to see her mother and her two brothers take the vessel for Norfolk, to be sold. This was the last time we ever saw her; we heard, sometime afterwards, that a kind master had bought her, and that she was doing well.

Many thrilling scenes I could relate, if necessary, that makes my blood curdle in my veins while I write. We were treated like cattle, subject to the slave-holders' brutal treatment and law.

The wretched condition of the male slave is bad enough; but that of the woman, driven to unremitting, unrequited toil, suffering, sick, and bearing the peculiar burdens of her own sex, unpitied, not assisted, as well as the toils which belong to another, must arouse the spirit of sympathy in every heart not dead to all feeling. Oh! how many heart-rending prayers I have heard ascend up to the throne of grace for deliverance from such exhibitions of barbarity. How many family ties have been broken by the cruel hand of slavery. The priceless store of pleasures, and the associations connected with home were unknown to the doomed slaves, for in an unlooked for hour they were sold to be separated from father and mother, brothers and sisters. Oh! how many such partings have rent many a heart, causing it to bleed as it were, and crushing out all hope of ever seeing slavery abolished.

Deliverance

Sometime before I left for the north, the land of freedom, I appointed another meeting in an off house on a plantation not far from Heathsville, where a number of us collected together to sing and pray. After I had given out the hymn, and prayed, I commenced to exhort the people. While I did so I became very warm and zealous in the work, and perhaps made more noise than we were aware of. The patrolers[1] going along the road, about half a mile off, heard the sound and followed it where we were holding our meeting. They came, armed to the teeth, and surrounded the house. The captain of the company came in, and as soon as we saw him we fell on our knees and prayed that God might deliver us. While we prayed he stood there in the middle of the floor,

---

1. The patrolers were southern spies, sent out, or were wont to roam at night to hunt up runaway slaves, and to investigate other matters.

without saying a word. Pretty soon we saw that his knees began to tremble, for it was too hot for him, so he turned and went out. His comrades asked him if "he was going to make an arrest"; he said "no, it was too hot there for him." They soon left, and that was the last we saw of them.

As God had delivered us in such a powerful manner, we took courage and held our meeting until day-break. Another time I had a meeting appointed at a freedwoman's house, whose name was Sister Gouldman, about five miles in the country. I left home about seven o'clock on Saturday evening, and arrived there about ten; we immediately commenced the meeting and continued it till about daylight. After closing the meeting we slept while Sister Gouldman was preparing the breakfast. After breakfast we went two miles further, and held another meeting till late in the afternoon, then closed and started for home, reaching there some time during the night. I was very much fatigued, and my energies were entirely exhausted, so much so that I was not able to work the next day.

The time when I was eighteen years old, when such a miraculous change had been wrought in my heart, I had had two holidays, and was up all night holding meetings, praying and singing most of the time. Not having any sleep, I could scarcely keep my eyes open when I went to work. While endeavoring to finish a piece of work, Mr. Lacky came and found me asleep while I was on my bench shoe-making. He told me that I had "been away enjoying myself for two days, and if he should come again and find me asleep, he would wake me up." Sure enough, he had no sooner left the shop when I was fast asleep again. As his shop was beneath mine, he could easily hear me when I was at work. He came up again in his stocking-feet, unawares, and the first thing I knew he had the rawhide, applying it vigorously to my flesh in such a manner that did not feel very pleasant to me. After punishing me, he asked me "if I thought I could keep awake after this." I told him "I thought possibly I could," and did, through a great deal of effort till night. I never was satisfied about that whipping.

Nat Turner's Confession

Nat Turner

Slave revolts were rare in North America, compared to other slaveholding regions such as the Caribbean and South America. The principal reasons include the fact that slaves in North America were more widely dispersed, forming a smaller percentage of the overall population than in slave-dominated places such as Haiti. In addition, North American slaves were under the close supervision of masters and overseers, who in contrast to Caribbean slaveowners lived and worked on their farms and plantations. Slaves in North America, at least during the colonial era, had no chance of attaining freedom by fleeing to the north or overseas, and could not escape capture while remaining close to home.

Yet North American slave revolts did take place, the largest of which was the Turner Rebellion of 1831. This rampage brought the deaths of fifty-nine whites in south-central Virginia and inspired a harsh repression throughout the southern slaveholding states that lasted for years. The leader of the uprising, the charismatic visionary Nat Turner, managed to escape search parties for six weeks after the rebellion was put down. After his capture, he was interviewed in his jail cell; knowing that he was doomed to certain execution, he made the following "Confession" of his religious visions and inspirations and of his actions during the revolt.

The Confession, Trial, and Execution of Nat Turner, the Negro Insurrectionist, Also a List of Persons Murdered in the Insurrection in Southampton County, Virginia, on the 21st and 22nd of August, 1831, with introductory remarks by T.R. Gray. (Petersburg, VA: J.B. Ege, 1881).

Y ou have asked me to give a history of the motives which induced me to undertake the late insurrection, as you call it—To do so I must go back to the days of my infancy, and even before I was born. I was thirty-one years of age the 2d of October last [1831], and born the property of Benj. Turner, of this county. In my childhood a circumstance occurred which made an indelible impression on my mind, and laid the ground work of that enthusiasm, which has terminated so fatally to many, both white and black, and for which I am about to atone at the gallows. It is here necessary to relate this circumstance—trifling as it may seem, it was the commencement of that belief which has grown with time, and even now, sir, in this dungeon, helpless and forsaken as I am, I cannot divest myself of. Being at play with other children, when three or four years old, I was telling them something, which my mother overhearing, said it had happened before I was born—I stuck to my story, however, and related somethings which went, in her opinion, to confirm it—others being called on were greatly astonished, knowing that these things had happened, and caused them to say in my hearing, I surely would be a prophet, as the Lord had shewn me things that had happened before my birth. And my father and mother strengthened me in this my first impression, saying in my presence, I was intended for some great purpose, which they had always thought from certain marks on my head and breast. . . .

Uncommon Intelligence

My grand mother, who was very religious, and to whom I was much attached—my master, who belonged to the church, and other religious persons who visited the house, and whom I often saw at prayers, noticing the singularity of my manners, I suppose, and my uncommon intelligence for a child, remarked I had too much sense to be raised, and if I was, I would never be of any service to any one as a slave—To a mind like mine, restless, inquisitive and observant of every thing that was passing, it is easy to suppose that religion was the subject to which it would be directed, and although this subject principally occupied my thoughts—there was nothing that I saw or heard of to which my attention was not directed—The manner in which I learned to read and write, not only had great influence on my own mind, as I acquired it with the most perfect ease, so much so, that I have no recollection whatever of learning the alphabet—but to the astonishment of the family, one day, when a book was shewn me to keep me from crying, I began spelling the names of different objects—this was a source of wonder to all in the neighborhood, particularly the blacks—and this learning was constantly improved at all opportunities—when I got large enough to go to work, while employed, I was reflecting on many things that would present themselves to my imagination, and whenever an opportunity occurred of looking at a book, when the school children were getting their lessons, I would find many things that the fertility of my own imagination had depicted to me before; all my time, not devoted to my master's service, was spent either in prayer, or in making experiments in casting different things in moulds made of earth, in attempting to make paper, gunpowder, and many other experiments, that although I could not perfect, yet convinced me of its practicability if I had the means. I was not addicted to stealing in my youth, nor have ever been—Yet such was the confidence of the negroes in the neighborhood, even at this early period of my life, in my superior judgment, that they would often carry me with them when they were going on any roguery, to plan for them. Growing up among them, with this confidence in my superior judgment, and when this, in their opinions, was perfected by Divine inspiration, from the circumstances already alluded to in my infancy, and which belief was ever afterwards zealously inculcated by the austerity of my life and manners, which became the subject of remark by white and black.—Having soon discovered to be great, I must appear so, and therefore studiously avoided mixing in society, and wrapped myself in mystery, devoting my time to fasting and prayer—

Fulfilling a Purpose

By this time, having arrived to man's estate, and hearing the scriptures commented on at meetings, I was struck with that particular passage which says: "Seek ye the kingdom of Heaven and all things shall be added unto you." I reflected much on this passage, and prayed daily for light on this subject—As I was praying one day at my plough, the spirit spoke to me, saying "Seek ye the kingdom of Heaven and all things shall be added unto you. Question [by Turner's interrogator]—what do you mean by the Spirit. Answer. The Spirit that spoke to the prophets in former days—and I was greatly astonished, and for two years prayed continually, whenever my duty would permit—and then again I had the same revelation, which fully confirmed me in the impression that I was ordained for some great purpose in the hands of the Almighty. Several years rolled round, in which many events occurred to strengthen me in this my belief. At this time I reverted in my mind to the remarks made of me in my childhood, and the things that had been shown me—and as it had been said of me in my childhood by those by whom I had been taught to pray, both white and black, and in whom I had the greatest confidence, that I had too much sense to be raised, and if I was, I would never be of any use to any one as a slave. Now finding I had arrived to man's estate, and was a slave, and these revelations being made known to me, I began to direct my attention to this great object, to fulfil the purpose for which, by this time, I felt assured I was intended. Knowing the influence I had obtained over the minds of my fellow servants, (not by the means of conjuring and such like tricks—for to them I always spoke of such things with contempt) but by the communion of the Spirit whose revelations I often communicated to them, and they believed and said my wisdom came from God. I now began to prepare them for my purpose, by telling them something was about to happen that would terminate in fulfilling the great promise that had been made to me—About this time I was placed under an overseer, from whom I ran away—and after remaining in the woods thirty days, I returned, to the astonishment of the negroes on the plantation, who thought I had made my escape to some other part of the country, as my father had done before. But the reason of my return was, that the Spirit appeared to me and said I had my wishes directed to the things of this world, and not to the kingdom of Heaven, and that I should return to the service of my earthly master—"For he who knoweth his Master's will, and doeth it not, shall be beaten with many stripes, and thus have I chastened you." And the negroes found fault, and murmured against me, saying that if they had my sense they would not serve any master in the world. And about this time I had a vision—and I saw white spirits and black spirits engaged in battle, and the sun was darkened—the thunder rolled in the Heavens, and blood flowed in streams—and I heard a voice saying, "Such is your luck, such you are called to see, and let it come rough or smooth, you must surely bare it."

Miracles

I now withdrew myself as much as my situation would permit, from the intercourse of my fellow servants, for the avowed purpose of serving the Spirit more fully—and it appeared to me, and reminded me of the things it had already shown me, and that it would then reveal to me the knowledge of the elements, the revolution of the planets, the operation of tides, and changes of the seasons. After this revelation in the year 1825, and the knowledge of the elements being made known to me, I sought more than ever to obtain true holiness before the great day of judgment should appear, and then I began to receive the true knowledge of faith. And from the first steps of righteousness until the last, was I made perfect; and the Holy Ghost was with me, and said, "Behold me as I stand in the Heavens"—and I looked and saw the forms of men in different attitudes—and there were lights in the sky to which the children of darkness gave other names than what they really were—for they were the lights of the Saviour's hands, stretched forth from east to west, even as they were extended on the cross on Calvary for the redemption of sinners. And I wondered greatly at these miracles, and prayed to be informed of a certainty of the meaning thereof—and shortly afterwards, while laboring in the field, I discovered drops of blood on the corn as though it were dew from heaven—and I communicated it to many, both white and black, in the neighborhood—and I then found on the leaves in the woods hieroglyphic characters, and numbers, with the forms of men in different attitudes, portrayed in blood, and representing the figures I had seen before in the heavens. And now the Holy Ghost had revealed itself to me, and made plain the miracles it had shown me—For as the blood of Christ had been shed on this earth, and had ascended to heaven for the salvation of sinners, and was now returning to earth again in the form of dew—and as the leaves on the trees bore the impression of the figures I had seen in the heavens, it was plain to me that the Saviour was about to lay down the yoke he had borne for the sins of men, and the great day of judgment was at hand. About this time I told these things to a white man, (Etheldred T. Brantley) on whom it had a wonderful effect—and he ceased from his wickedness, and was attacked immediately with a cutaneous eruption, and blood oozed from the pores of his skin, and after praying and fasting nine days, he was healed, and the Spirit appeared to me again, and said, as the Saviour had been baptised so should we be also—and when the white people would not let us be baptised by the church, we went down into the water together, in the sight of many who reviled us, and were baptised by the Spirit—After this I rejoiced greatly, and gave thanks to God. And on the 12th of May, 1828, 1 heard a loud noise in the heavens, and the Spirit instantly appeared to me and said the Serpent was loosened, and Christ had laid down the yoke he had borne for the sins of men, and that I should take it on and fight against the Serpent, for the time was fast approaching when the first should be last and the last should be first. Question. Do you not find yourself mistaken now? Answer. Was not Christ crucified. And by signs in the heavens that it would make known to me when I should commence the great work—and until the first sign appeared, I should conceal it from the knowledge of men—And on the appearance of the sign, (the eclipse of the sun last February) I should arise and prepare myself, and slay my enemies with their own weapons. And immediately on the sign appearing in the heavens, the seal was removed from my lips, and I communicated the great work laid out for me to do, to four in whom I had the greatest confidence, (Henry, Hark, Nelson, and Sam)—it was intended by us to have begun the work of death on the 4th July last—Many were the plans formed and rejected by us, and it affected my mind to such a degree, that I fell sick, and the time passed without our coming to any determination how to commence—Still forming new schemes and rejecting them, when the sign appeared again, which determined me not to wait longer.

Laying the Plan

Since the commencement of 1830, I had been living with Mr. Joseph Travis, who was to me a kind master, and placed the greatest confidence in me; in fact, I had no cause to complain of his treatment to me. On Saturday evening, the 20th of August, it was agreed between Henry, Hark and myself, to prepare a dinner the next day for the men we expected, and then to concert a plan, as we had not yet determined on any. Hark, on the following morning, brought a pig, and Henry brandy, and being joined by Sam, Nelson, Will and Jack, they prepared in the woods a dinner, where, about three o'clock, I joined them.

Question. Why were you so backward in joining them.

Answer. The same reason that had caused me not to mix with them for years before.

I saluted them on coming up, and asked Will how came he there, he answered, his life was worth no more than others, and his liberty as dear to him. I asked him if he thought to obtain it? He said he would, or loose [sic] his life. This was enough to put him in full confidence. Jack, I knew, was only a tool in the hands of Hark, it was quickly agreed we should commence at home (Mr. J. Travis') on that night, and until we had armed and equipped ourselves, and gathered sufficient force, neither age nor sex was to be spared, (which was invariably adhered to.) We remained at the feast, until about two hours in the night, when we went to the house and found Austin; they all went to the cider press and drank, except myself. On returning to the house, Hark went to the door with an axe, for the purpose of breaking it open, as we knew we were strong enough to murder the family, if they were awaked by the noise; but reflecting that it might create an alarm in the neighborhood, we determined to enter the house secretly, and murder them whilst sleeping. Hark got a ladder and set it against the chimney, on which I ascended, and hoisting a window, entered and came down stairs, unbarred the door, and removed the guns from their places. It was then observed that I must spill the first blood. On which, armed with a hatchet, and accompanied by Will, I entered my master's chamber, it being dark, I could not give a death blow, the hatchet glanced from his head, he sprang from the bed and called his wife, it was his last work, Will laid him dead, with a blow of his axe, and Mrs. Travis shared the same fate, as she lay in bed. The murder of this family, five in number, was the work of a moment, not one of them awoke; there was a little infant sleeping in a cradle, that was forgotten, until we had left the house and gone some distance, when Henry and Will returned and killed it; we got here, four guns that would shoot, and several old muskets, with a pound or two of powder. We remained some time at the barn, where we paraded; I formed them in a line as soldiers, and after carrying them through all the manoeuvres I was master of, marched them off to Mr. Salathul Francis', about six hundred yards distant. Sam and Will went to the door and knocked. Mr. Francis asked who was there, Sam replied it was him, and he had a letter for him, on which he got up and came to the door; they immediately seized him, and dragging him out a little from the door, he was dispatched by repeated blows on the head; there was no other white person in the family. We started from there for Mrs. Reese's, maintaining the most perfect silence on our march, where finding the door unlocked, we entered, and murdered Mrs. Reese in her bed, while sleeping; her son awoke, but it was only to sleep the sleep of death, he had only time to say who is that, and he was no more. From Mrs. Reese's we went to Mrs. Turner's, a mile distant, which we reached about sunrise, on Monday morning. Henry, Austin, and Sam, went to the still, where, finding Mr. Peebles, Austin shot him, and the rest of us went to the house; as we approached, the family discovered us, and shut the door. Vain hope! Will, with one stroke of his axe, opened it, and we entered and found Mrs. Turner and Mrs. Newsome in the middle of a room, almost frightened to death. Will immediately killed Mrs. Turner, with one blow of his axe. I took Mrs. Newsome by the hand, and with the sword I had when I was apprehended, I struck her several blows over the head, but not being able to kill her, as the sword was dull. Will, turning around and discovering it, despatched her also. A general destruction of property and search for money and ammunition, always succeeded the murders.

Spreading Alarm

By this time my company amounted to fifteen, and nine men mounted, who started for Mrs. Whitehead's, (the other six were to go through a by way to Mr. Bryant's, and rejoin us at Mrs. Whitehead's,) as we approached the house we discovered Mr. Richard Whitehead standing in the cotton patch, near the lane fence; we called him over into the lane, and Will, the executioner, was near at hand, with his fatal axe, to send him to an untimely grave. As we pushed on to the house, I discovered some one run round the garden, and thinking it was some of the white family, I pursued them, but finding it was a servant girl belonging to the house, I returned to commence the work of death, but they whom I left, had not been idle; all the family were already murdered, but Mrs. Whitehead and her daughter Margaret. As I came round to the door I saw Will pulling Mrs. Whitehead out of the house, and at the step he nearly severed her head from her body, with his broad axe. Miss Margaret, when I discovered her, had concealed herself in the corner, formed by the projection of the cellar cap from the house; on my approach she fled, but was soon overtaken, and after repeated blows with a sword, I killed her by a blow on the head, with a fence rail. By this time, the six who had gone by Mr. Bryant's, rejoined us, and informed me they had done the work of death assigned them. We again divided, part going to Mr. Richard Porter's, and from thence to Nathaniel Francis', the others to Mr. Howell Harris', and Mr. T. Doyle's. On my reaching Mr. Porter's, he had escaped with his family. I understood there, that the alarm had already spread, and I immediately returned to bring up those sent to Mr. Doyle's, and Mr. Howell Harris'; the party I left going on to Mr. Francis', having told them I would join them in that neighborhood. I met these sent to Mr. Doyle's and Mr. Harris' returning, having met Mr. Doyle on the road and killed him; and learning from some who joined them, that Mr. Harris was from home, I immediately pursued the course taken by the party gone on before; but knowing they would complete the work of death and pillage, at Mr. Francis' before I could get there, I went to Mr. Peter Edwards', expecting to find them there, but they had been here also. I then went to Mr. John T. Barrow's, they had been here and murdered him. I pursued on their track to Capt. Newit Harris', where I found the greater part mounted, and ready to start; the men now amounting to about forty, shouted and hurraed as I rode up, some were in the yard, loading their guns, others drinking. They said Captain Harris and his family had escaped, the property in the house they destroyed, robbing him of money and other valuables. I ordered them to mount and march instantly, this was about nine or ten o'clock, Monday morning. I proceeded to Mr. Levi Waller's, two or three miles distant. I took my station in the rear, and as it 'twas my object to carry terror and devastation wherever we went, I placed fifteen or twenty of the best armed and most to be relied on, in front, who generally approached the houses as fast as their horses could run; this was for two purposes, to prevent their escape and strike terror to the inhabitants—on this account I never got to the houses, after leaving Mrs. Whitehead's, until the murders were committed, except in one case. I sometimes got in sight in time to see the work of death completed, viewed the mangled bodies as they lay, in silent satisfaction, and immediately started in quest of other victims—Having murdered Mrs. Waller and ten children, we started for Mr. William Williams'—having killed him and two little boys that were there; while engaged in this, Mrs. Williams fled and got some distance from the house, but she was pursued, overtaken, and compelled to get up behind one of the company, who brought her back, and after showing her the mangled body of her lifeless husband, she was told to get down and lay by his side, where she was shot dead. I then started for Mr. Jacob Williams, where the family were murdered—Here we found a young man named Drury, who had come on business with Mr. Williams—he was pursued, overtaken and shot. Mrs. Vaughan was the next place we visited—and after murdering the family here, I determined on starting for Jerusalem—Our number amounted now to fifty or sixty, all mounted and armed with guns, axes, swords and clubs—On reaching Mr. James W. Parker's gate, immediately on the road leading to Jerusalem, and about three miles distant, it was proposed to me to call there, but I objected, as I knew he was gone to Jerusalem, and my object was to reach there as soon as possible; but some of the men having relations at Mr. Parker's it was agreed that they might call and get his people. I remained at the gate on the road, with seven or eight; the others going across the field to the house, about half a mile off. After waiting some time for them, I became impatient, and started to the house for them, and on our return we were met by a party of white men, who had pursued our blood-stained track, and who had fired on those at the gate, and dispersed them, which I knew nothing of, not having been at that time rejoined by any of them—Immediately on discovering the whites, I ordered my men to halt and form, as they appeared to be alarmed—

Turner's Escape

The white men, eighteen in number, approached us in about one hundred yards, when one of them fired, (this was against the positive orders of Captain Alexander P. Peete, who commanded, and who had directed the men to reserve their fire until within thirty paces) And I discovered about half of them retreating, I then ordered my men to fire and rush on them; the few remaining stood their ground until we approached within fifty yards, when they fired and retreated. We pursued and overtook some of them who we thought we left dead; . . . after pursuing them about two hundred yards, and rising a little hill, I discovered they were met by another party, and had halted, and were re-loading their guns. . . . Thinking that those who retreated first, and the party who fired on us at fifty or sixty yards distant, had all only fallen back to meet others with ammunition. As I saw them re-loading their guns, and more coming up than I saw at first, and several of my bravest men being wounded, the others became panick [sic] struck and squandered over the field; the white men pursued and fired on us several times. Hark had his horse shot under him, and I caught another for him as it was running by me; five or six of my men were wounded, but none left on the field; finding myself defeated here I instantly determined to go through a private way, and cross the Nottoway river at the Cypress Bridge, three miles below Jerusalem, and attack that place in the rear, as I expected they would look for me on the other road, and I had a great desire to get there to procure arms and ammunition. After going a short distance in this private way, accompanied by about twenty men, I overtook two or three who told me the others were dispersed in every direction. After trying in vain to collect a sufficient force to proceed to Jerusalem, I determined to return, as I was sure they would make back to their old neighborhood, where they would rejoin me, make new recruits, and come down again. On my way back, I called at Mrs. Thomas's, Mrs. Spencer's, and several other places, the white families having fled, we found no more victims to gratify our thirst for blood, we stopped at Majr. Ridley's quarter for the night, and being joined by four of his men, with the recruits made since my defeat, we mustered now about forty strong. After placing out sentinels, I laid down to sleep, but was quickly roused by a great racket; starting up, I found some mounted, and others in great confusion; one of the sentinels having given the alarm that we were about to be attacked, I ordered some to ride round and reconnoitre, and on their return the others being more alarmed, not knowing who they were, fled in different ways, so that I was reduced to about twenty again; with this I determined to attempt to recruit, and proceed on to rally in the neighborhood, I had left. Dr. Blunt's was the nearest house, which we reached just before day; on riding up the yard, Hark fired a gun. We expected Dr. Blunt and his family were at Maj. Ridley's, as I knew there was a company of men there; the gun was fired to ascertain if any of the family were at home; we were immediately fired upon and retreated, leaving several of my men. I do not know what became of them, as I never saw them afterwards. Pursuing our course back and coming in sight of Captain Harris', where we had been the day before, we discovered a party of white men at the house, on which all deserted me but two, (Jacob and Nat,) we concealed ourselves in the woods until near night, when I sent them in search of Henry, Sam, Nelson, and Hark, and directed them to rally all they could, at the place we had had our dinner the Sunday before, where they would find me, and I accordingly returned there as soon as it was dark and remained until Wednesday evening, when discovering white men riding around the place as though they were looking for some one, and none of my men joining me, I concluded Jacob and Nat had been taken, and compelled to betray me. On this I gave up all hope for the present; and on Thursday night after having supplied myself with provisions from Mr. Travis's, I scratched a hole under a pile of fence rails in a field, where I concealed myself for six weeks, never leaving my hiding place but for a few minutes in the dead of night to get water which was very near; thinking by this time I could venture out, I began to go about in the night and eaves drop [sic] the houses in the neighborhood; pursuing this course for about a fortnight and gathering little or no intelligence, afraid of speaking to any human being, and returning every morning to my cave before the dawn of day. I know not how long I might have led this life, if accident had not betrayed me, a dog in the neighborhood passing by my hiding place one night while I was out, was attracted by some meat I had in my cave, and crawled in and stole it, and was coming out just as I returned. A few nights after; two negroes having started to go hunting with the same dog, and passed that way, the dog came again to the place, and having just gone out to walk about, discovered me and barked, on which thinking myself discovered, I spoke to them to beg concealment. On making myself known they fled from me. Knowing then they would betray me, I immediately left my hiding place, and was pursued almost incessantly until I was taken a fortnight afterwards by Mr. Benjamin Phipps, in a little hole I had dug out with my sword, for the purpose of concealment, under the top of a fallen tree. On Mr. Phipps' discovering the place of my concealment, he cocked his gun and aimed at me. I requested him not to shoot and I would give up, upon which he demanded my sword. I delivered it to him, and he brought me to prison. During the time I was pursued, I had many hair breadth escapes, which your time will not permit you to relate. I am here loaded with chains, and willing to suffer the fate that awaits me.

An Escape Betrayed

Frederick Douglass

> Frederick Douglass escaped from slavery to become one of
> the leading black writers and lecturers in the United States.
> Born in Maryland of an unknown white father and a black
> mother, he taught himself to read and write while still a boy
> in captivity, giving himself a crucial advantage when he
> finally fled to Massachusetts and freedom at the age of
> twenty one. After becoming a member of the Massachusetts
> Anti-Slavery Society, Douglass made thousands of converts
> to abolitionism through his eloquent writings and speeches.
>
> Although he won a wide audience in New England, Dou-
> glass also attracted critics who could not believe he had ever
> been a slave. To refute these rumors, he published the story of
> his youth—an account that proved as convincing as his lec-
> tures, and which threatened his own imprisonment and return
> to the South as an escaped slave. Douglass fled to Britain in
> 1845 but eventually earned enough from his lectures to buy
> his freedom and return to the United States.
>
> In 1855, Douglass returned to his own youth in *My
> Bondage and My Freedom.* In this book he recounts one of
> his own schemes for escape from his owners. As Douglass's
> account makes clear, the hopeful runaway faced a long list of
> dangers when considering escape; uppermost among them
> was the betrayal of fellow conspirators seeking the favor of
> their masters.

I had succeeded in winning to my scheme a company of
five young men, the very flower of the neighborhood,
each one of whom would have commanded one thousand

From Frederick Douglass, *My Bondage and My Freedom* (New York: Miller, Orton &
Mulligan, 1855).

dollars in the home market. At New Orleans they would have brought fifteen hundred dollars apiece, and perhaps more. Their names were as follows: Henry Harris, John Harris, Sandy Jenkins, Charles Roberts, and Henry Bailey. I was the youngest but one of the party. I had, however, the advantage of them all in experience, and in a knowledge of letters. This gave me a great influence over them. Perhaps not one of them, left to himself, would have dreamed of escape as a possible thing. They all wanted to be free, but the serious thought of running away had not entered into their minds until I won them to the undertaking. They were all tolerably well off—for slaves—and had dim hopes of being set free some day by their masters. If any one is to blame for disturbing the quiet of the slaves and slave-masters of the neighborhood of St. Michaels, I AM THE MAN. I claim to be the instigator of the high crime (as the slaveholders regarded it), and I kept life in it till life could be kept in it no longer.

Pending the time of our contemplated departure out of our Egypt, we met often by night, and on every Sunday. At these meetings we talked the matter over, told our hopes and fears, and the difficulties discovered or imagined; and, like men of sense, counted the cost of the enterprise to which we were committing ourselves. These meetings must have resembled, on a small scale, the meetings of the revolutionary conspirators in their primary condition. We were plotting against our (so-called) lawful rulers, with this difference—we sought our own good, and not the harm of our enemies. We did not seek to overthrow them, but to escape from them. As for Mr. Freeland, [one of Douglass's masters] we all liked him, and would gladly have remained with him as *free men. Liberty* was our aim, and we had now come to think that we had a right to it against every obstacle, even against the lives of our enslavers.

We had several words, expressive of things important to us, which we understood, but which, even if distinctly heard by an outsider, would have conveyed no certain meaning. I hated this secrecy, but where slavery was powerful, and liberty weak, the latter was driven to concealment or destruction.

The prospect was not always bright. At times we were almost tempted to abandon the enterprise, and to try to get back to that comparative peace of mind, which even a man under the gallows might feel when all hope of escape had vanished. We were, at times, confident, bold and determined, and again, doubting, timid and wavering; whistling, as did the boy in the grave-yard to keep away the spirits.

Notions of Geography

To look at the map and observe the proximity of Eastern shore, Maryland, to Delaware and Pennsylvania, it may seem to the reader quite absurd to regard the proposed escape as a formidable undertaking. But to *understand,* someone has said, a man must *stand under.* The real distance was great enough, but the imagined distance was, to our ignorance, much greater. Slaveholders sought to impress their slaves with a belief in the boundlessness of slave territory, and of their own limitless power. Our notions of the geography of the country were very vague and indistinct. The distance, however, was not the chief trouble, for the nearer were the lines of a slave state to the borders of a free state the greater was the trouble. Hired kidnappers infested the borders. Then, too, we knew that merely reaching a free state did not free us, that wherever caught we could be returned to slavery. We knew of no spot this side of the ocean where we could be safe. We had heard of Canada, then the only real Canaan of the American bondman, simply as a country to which the wild goose and the swan repaired at the end of winter to escape the heat of summer, but not as the home of man. I knew something of theology, but nothing of geography. I really did not know that there was a State of New York, or a State of Massachusetts. I had heard of Pennsylvania, Delaware, and New Jersey, and all the Southern States, but was utterly ignorant of the free States. New York City was our northern limit, and to go there and to be forever harassed with the liability of being hunted down and returned to slavery, with the certainty of being treated ten times worse than ever before, was a prospect

which might well cause some hesitation. The case sometimes, to our excited visions, stood thus: At every gate
through which we had to pass we saw a watchman; at every
ferry a guard; on every bridge a sentinel, and in every wood
a patrol or slave-hunter. We were hemmed in on every side.
The good to be sought and the evil to be shunned were flung
in the balance and weighed against each other. On the one
hand stood slavery, a stern reality glaring frightfully upon
us, with the blood of millions in its polluted skirts, terrible
to behold, greedily devouring our hard earnings and feeding
upon our flesh. This was the evil from which to escape. On
the other hand, far away, back in the hazy distance where all
forms seemed but shadows under the flickering light of the
north star, behind some craggy hill or snow-capped moun-
tain, stood a doubtful freedom, half frozen, and beckoning
us to her icy domain. This was the good to be sought. The
inequality was as great as that between certainty and uncertainty. This in itself was enough to stagger us; but when we
came to survey the untrodden road and conjecture the many
possible difficulties, we were appalled, and at times, as I
have said, were upon the point of giving over the struggle
altogether. The reader can have little idea of the phantoms
which would flit, in such circumstances, before the unedu-
cated mind of the slave. Upon either side we saw grim
death, assuming a variety of horrid shapes. Now it was star-
vation, causing us, in a strange and friendless land, to eat
our own flesh. Now we were contending with the waves and
were drowned. Now we were hunted by dogs and overtak-
en, and torn to pieces by their merciless fangs. We were
stung by scorpions, chased by wild beasts, bitten by snakes,
and, worst of all, after having succeeded in swimming
rivers, encountering wild beasts, sleeping in the woods, and
suffering hunger, cold, heat and nakedness, were overtaken
by hired kidnappers, who, in the name of law and for the
thrice-cursed reward, would, perchance, fire upon us, kill
some, wound others and capture all. This dark picture,
drawn by ignorance and fear, at times greatly shook our determination, and not unfrequently caused us to

"Rather bear the ills we had,
Than flee to others which we knew not of."

I am not disposed to magnify this circumstance in my experience, and yet I think that, to the reader, I shall seem to be so disposed. But no man can tell the intense agony which was felt by the slave when wavering on the point of making his escape. All that he has is at stake, and even that which he has not is at stake also. The life which he has may be lost and the liberty which he seeks may not be gained.

Hesitation and a Bad Dream

Patrick Henry, to a listening senate which was thrilled by his magic eloquence and ready to stand by him in his boldest flights, could say, "Give me liberty or give me death"; and this saying was a sublime one, even for a freeman; but incomparably more sublime is the same sentiment when *practically* asserted by men accustomed to the lash and chain, men whose sensibilities must have become more or less deadened by their bondage. With us it was a doubtful liberty, at best, that we sought, and a certain lingering death in the rice-swamps and sugar-fields if we failed. Life is not lightly regarded by men of sane minds. It is precious both to the pauper and to the prince, to the slave and to his master; and yet I believe there was not one among us who would not rather have been shot down than pass away life in hopeless bondage.

In the progress of our preparations Sandy (the root man) became troubled. He began to have distressing dreams. One of these, which happened on a Friday night, was to him of great significance, and I am quite ready to confess that I myself felt somewhat damped by it. He said: "I dreamed last night that I was roused from sleep by strange noises, like the noises of a swarm of angry birds that caused as they passed, a roar which fell upon my ear like a coming gale over the tops of the trees. Looking up to see what it could mean, I saw you, Frederick, in the claws of a huge bird, surrounded by a large number of birds of all colors and sizes. These were all pecking at you, while you, with your arms, seemed to be trying to protect your eyes. Passing over me, the birds flew in a southwesterly direction, and I watched them until they were clean out of sight. Now I saw this as plainly as I now see you; and furder, honey, watch de Friday night dream; dere is sumpon in it shose you born; dere is indeed, honey." I did not like the dream, but I showed no concern, attributing it to the general excitement and perturbation consequent upon our contemplated plan to escape. I could not, however, at once shake off its effect. I felt that it boded no good. Sandy was unusually emphatic and oracular and his manner had much to do with the impression made upon me.

The Plan

The plan for our escape, which I recommended and to which my comrades consented, was to take a large canoe owned by Mr. Hamilton, and on the Saturday night previous to the Easter holidays launch out into the Chesapeake bay and paddle with all our might for its head, a distance of seventy miles. On reaching this point we were to turn the canoe adrift and bend our steps toward the north-star till we reached a free state.

There were several objections to this plan. In rough weather the waters of the Chesapeake are much agitated, and there would be danger, in a canoe, of being swamped by the waves. Another objection was that the canoe would soon be missed, the absent slaves would at once be suspected of having taken it, and we should be pursued by some of the fast-sailing craft out of St. Michaels. Then again, if we reached the head of the bay and turned the canoe adrift, she might prove a guide to our track and bring the hunters after us.

These and other objections were set aside by the stronger ones, which could be urged against every other plan that could then be suggested. On the water we had a chance of being regarded as fishermen, in the service of a master. On the other hand, by taking the land route, through the counties adjoining Delaware, we should be subjected to all manner of interruptions, and many disagreeable questions, which might give us serious trouble. Any white man, if he pleased, was authorized to stop a man of color on any road, and examine and arrest him. By this arrangement many abuses (considered such even by slaveholders) occurred. Cases have been known where freemen, being called upon by a pack of ruffians to show their free papers, have presented them, when the ruffians have torn them up, seized the victim and sold him to a life of endless bondage.

The week before our intended start, I wrote a pass for each of our party, giving him permission to visit Baltimore during the Easter holidays. The pass ran after this manner:

> "This is to certify that I, the undersigned, have given the bearer, my servant John, full liberty to go to Baltimore to spend the Easter holidays.   W.H.
> NEAR ST. MICHAELS, Talbot Co., Md."

Although we were not going to Baltimore, and were intending to land east of North Point, in the direction I had seen the Philadelphia steamers go, these passes might be useful to us in the lower part of the bay, while steering towards Baltimore. These were not, however, to be shown by us until all our answers had failed to satisfy the inquirer. We were all fully alive to the importance of being calm and self-possessed when accosted, if accosted we should be; and we more than once rehearsed to each other how we should behave in the hour of trial.

Those were long, tedious days and nights. The suspense was painful in the extreme. To balance probabilities, where life and liberty hang on the result, requires steady nerves. I panted for action, and was glad when the day, at the close of which we were to start, dawned upon us. Sleeping, the night before, was out of the question. I probably felt more deeply than any of my companions, because I was the instigator of the movement. The responsibility of the whole enterprise rested upon my shoulders. The glory of success and the shame and confusion of failure, could not be matters of indifference to me. Our food was prepared, our clothes were packed; we were already to go, and impatient for Saturday morning—considering *that* the last of our bondage.

The Time Draws Near

I cannot describe the tempest and tumult of my brain that morning. The reader will please bear in mind that in a slave State an unsuccessful runaway was not only subjected to cruel torture, and sold away to the far South, but he was frequently execrated by the other slaves. He was charged with making the condition of the other slaves intolerable by laying them all under the suspicion of their masters—subjecting them to greater vigilance, and imposing greater limitations on their privileges. I dreaded murmurs from this quarter. It was difficult, too, for a slave-master to believe that slaves escaping had not been aided in their flight by some one of their fellow-slaves. When, therefore, a slave was missing, every slave on the place was closely examined as to his knowledge of the undertaking.

Our anxiety grew more and more intense, as the time of our intended departure drew nigh. It was truly felt to be a matter of life and death with us, and we fully intended to *fight*, as well as *run*, if necessity should occur for that extremity. But the trial-hour had not yet come. It was easy to resolve, but not so easy to act. I expected there might be some drawing back at the last; it was natural there should be; therefore, during the intervening time, I lost no opportunity to explain away difficulties, remove doubts, dispel fears, and inspire all with firmness. It was too late to look back, and now was the time to go forward. I appealed to the pride of my comrades by telling them that if, after having solemnly promised to go, as they had done, they now failed to make the attempt, they would in effect brand themselves with cowardice, and might well sit down, fold their arms, and acknowledge themselves fit only to be slaves. This detestable character all were unwilling to assume. Every man except Sandy (he, much to our regret, withdrew) stood firm, and at our last meeting we pledged ourselves afresh, and in the most solemn manner, that at the time appointed we *would* certainly start on our long journey for a free country. This meeting was in the middle of the week, at the end of which we were to start.

A Bad Feeling

Early on the appointed morning we went as usual to the field, but with hearts that beat quickly and anxiously. Any one intimately acquainted with us might have seen that all was not well with us, and that some monster lingered in our thoughts. Our work that morning was the same that it had been for several days past—drawing out and spreading manure. While thus engaged, I had a sudden presentiment, which flashed upon me like lightning in a dark night, revealing to the lonely traveler the gulf before and the enemy behind. I instantly turned to Sandy Jenkins, who was near me, and said: *"Sandy, we are betrayed!*—something has just told me so." I felt as sure of it as if the officers were in sight. Sandy said: "Man, dat is strange; but I feel just as you do." If my mother—then long in her grave—had appeared before me and told me that we were betrayed, I could not at that moment have felt more certain of the fact.

In a few minutes after this, the long, low, and distant notes of the horn summoned us from the field to breakfast. I felt as one may be supposed to feel before being led forth to be executed for some great offense. I wanted no breakfast, but for form's sake I went with the other slaves toward the house. My feelings were not disturbed as to the right of running away; on that point I had no misgiving whatever, but from a sense of the consequences of failure.

The Arrest

In thirty minutes after that vivid impression came the apprehended crash. On reaching the house, and glancing my eye toward the lane gate, the worst was at once made known. The lane gate to Mr. Freeland's house was nearly half a mile from the door, and much shaded by the heavy wood which bordered the main road. I was, however, able to descry four white men and two colored men approaching. The white men were on horseback, and the colored men were walking behind, and seemed to be tied. "*It is indeed all over with us; we are surely betrayed,*" I thought to myself. I became composed, or at least comparatively so, and calmly awaited the result. I watched the ill-omened company entering the gate. Successful flight was impossible, and I made up my mind to

Rewards

Slaves were valuable property; a young, healthy slave could bring more than one thousand dollars at a Southern slave auction. For this reason, owners went to great lengths to retrieve slaves whenever they ran away. The following advertisement is typical of the reward offers that appeared in Southern newspapers through the eighteenth and nineteenth centuries.

100 DOLLS. REWARD.

RAN AWAY

From me, on Saturday, the 19th inst.,

Negro Boy Robert Porter,

aged 19; heavy, stoutly made; dark chesnut complexion; rather sullen countenance,

with a down look; face large; head low on the shoulders. I believe he entered the City of Washington on Sunday evening, 20th inst. He has changed his dress probably, except his boots, which were new and heavy.

I will give $50 if taken and secured in the District of Columbia, or $100 if taken north of the District, and secured in each case and delivered before the reward shall be good.

Dr. J. W. THOMAS.

Pomunky P.O., Charles Co., MD.

stand and meet the evil, whatever it might be, for I was not altogether without a slight hope that things might turn differently from what I had at first feared. In a few moments in came Mr. William Hamilton, riding very rapidly and evidently much excited. He was in the habit of riding very slowly, and was seldom known to gallop his horse. This time his horse was nearly at full speed, causing the dust to roll thick behind him. Mr. Hamilton, though one of the most resolute men in the whole neighborhood, was, nevertheless, a remarkably mild-spoken man, and even when greatly excited his language was cool and circumspect. He came to the door, and inquired if Mr. Freeland was in. I told him that Mr. Freeland was at the barn. Off the old gentleman rode toward the barn, with unwonted speed. In a few moments Mr. Hamilton and Mr. Freeland came down from the barn to the house, and just as they made their appearance in the front-yard, three men, who proved to be constables, came dashing into the lane on horseback, as if summoned by a sign requiring quick work. A few seconds brought them into the front-yard, where they hastily dismounted and tied their horses. This done, they joined Mr. Freeland and Mr. Hamilton, who were standing a short distance from the kitchen. A few moments were spent as if in consulting how to proceed, and then the whole party walked up to the kitchen-door. There was now no one in the kitchen but myself and John Harris; Henry and Sandy were yet in the barn. Mr. Freeland came inside the kitchen-door, and, with an agitated voice, called me by name, and told me to come forward; that there were some gentlemen who wished to see me. I stepped toward them at the door, and asked what they wanted; when the constables grabbed me, and told me that I had better not resist; that I had been in a scrape, or was said to have been in one; that they were merely going to take me where I could be examined; that they would have me brought before my master at St. Michaels, and if the evidence against me was not proved true I should be acquitted. I was now firmly tied, and completely at the mercy of my captors. Resistance was idle. They were five in number and armed to the teeth. When they had secured me, they turned to John Harris and in a few moments succeeded in tying him as firmly as they had tied me. They next turned toward Henry Harris, who had now returned from the barn. "Cross your hands," said the constable to Henry. "I won't," said Henry, in a voice so firm and clear, and in a manner so determined, as for a moment to arrest all proceedings. "Won't you cross your hands?" said Tom Graham, the constable. "*No, I won't*," said Henry, with increasing emphasis. Mr. Hamilton, Mr. Freeland, and the officers now came near to Henry. Two of the constables drew out their shining pistols, and swore, by the name of God, that he should cross his hands or they would shoot him down. Each of these hired ruffians now cocked his pistol, and, with fingers apparently on the triggers, presented his deadly weapon to the breast of the unarmed slave, saying, that if he did not cross his hands, he would "blow his d—d heart out of him." *"Shoot me, shoot me,"* said Henry; "you can't kill me but once. *Shoot, shoot,* and be damned! I won't be tied!" This the brave fellow said in a voice as defiant and heroic in its tone as was the language itself; and at the moment of saying it, with the pistols at his very breast, he quickly raised his arms and dashed them from the puny hands of his assassins, the weapons flying in all directions. Now came the struggle. All hands rushed upon the brave fellow and after beating him for some time succeeded in overpowering and tying him. Henry put me to shame; he fought, and fought bravely. John and I had made no resistance. The fact is, I never saw much use of fighting where there was no reasonable probability of whipping anybody. Yet there was something almost providential in the resistance made by Henry. But for that resistance every soul of us would have been hurried off to the far South. Just a moment previous to the trouble with Henry, Mr. Hamilton *mildly* said,—and this gave me the unmistakable clue to the cause of our arrest,—"Perhaps we had now better make a search for those protections [passes], which we understand Frederick has written for himself and the rest." Had these passes been found, they would have been point-blank evidence against us, and would have confirmed all the statements of our betrayer. Thanks to the resistance of Henry, the excitement produced by the scuffle drew all attention in that direction, and I succeeded in flinging my pass, unobserved, into the fire. The confusion attendant on the scuffle, and the apprehension of still further trouble, perhaps, led our captors to forego, for the time, any search for *"those protections* which Frederick was said to have written for his companions"; so we were not yet convicted of the purpose to run away, and it was evident that there was some doubt on the part of all whether we had been guilty of such purpose.

Just as we were all completely tied, and about ready to start toward St. Michaels, and thence to jail, Mrs. Betsey Freeland (mother to William, who was much attached, after the Southern fashion, to Henry and John, they having been reared from childhood in her house) came to the kitchen-door with her hands full of biscuits, for we had not had our breakfast that morning, and divided them between Henry and John. This done, the lady made the following parting address to me, pointing her bony finger at me: "You devil! you yellow devil! It was you who put it into the heads of Henry and John to run away. But for *you, you long-legged, yellow devil,* Henry and John would never have thought of running away." I gave the lady a look which called forth from her a scream of mingled wrath and terror, as she slammed the kitchen-door and went in, leaving me, with the rest, in hands as harsh as her own broken voice.

In the Hands of Vultures

Could the kind reader have been riding along the main road to or from Easton that morning, his eye would have met a painful sight. He would have seen five young men, guilty of no crime save that of preferring *liberty* to *slavery*, drawn along the public highway—firmly bound together, tramping through dust and heat, bare-footed and bare-headed—fastened to three strong horses, whose riders were armed with pistols and daggers, and on their way to prison like felons, and suffering every possible insult from the crowds of idle, vulgar people who clustered round, and heartlessly made their failure to escape the occasion for all manner of ribaldry and sport. As I looked upon this crowd of vile persons, and saw myself and friends thus assailed and persecuted, I could not help seeing the fulfillment of Sandy's dream. I was in the hands of moral vultures, and held in their sharp talons, and was being hurried away toward Easton, in a south-easterly direction, amid the jeers of new birds of the same feather, through every neighborhood we passed. It seemed to me that everybody was out, and knew the cause of our arrest, and awaited our passing in order to feast their vindictive eyes on our misery.

Some said "*I ought to be hanged,*" and others, "*I ought to be burned*"; others, I ought to have the "hide" taken off my back; while no one gave us a kind word or sympathizing look, except the poor slaves who were lifting their heavy hoes, and who cautiously glanced at us through the post-and-rail fences, behind which they were at work. Our sufferings that morning can be more easily imagined than described. Our hopes were all blasted at one blow. The cruel injustice, the victorious crime, and the helplessness of innocence, led me to ask in my ignorance and weakness: Where is now the God of justice and mercy? and why have these wicked men the power thus to trample upon our rights, and to insult our feelings? and yet in the next moment came the consoling thought, "the day of the oppressor will come at last." Of one thing I could be glad: not one of my dear friends upon whom I had brought this great calamity, reproached me, either by word or look, for having led them into it. We were a band of brothers, and never dearer to each other than now. The thought which gave us the most pain was the probable separation which would now take place in case we were sold off to the far South, as we were likely to be. While the constables were looking forward, Henry and I being fastened together, could occasionally exchange a word without being observed by the kidnappers who had us in charge. "What shall I do with my pass?" said Henry. "Eat it with your biscuit," said I; "it won't do to tear it up." We were now near St. Michaels. The direction concerning the passes was passed around, and executed. "Own [admit] nothing," said I. "Own nothing" was passed round, enjoined, and assented to. Our confidence in each other was unshaken, and we were quite resolved to succeed or fail together; as much after the calamity which had befallen us as before.

The Suspected Betrayer

On reaching St. Michaels we underwent a sort of examination at my master's store, and it was evident to my mind that Master Thomas suspected the truthfulness of the evidence upon which they had acted in arresting us, and that he only affected, to some extent, the positiveness with which he asserted our guilt. There was nothing said by any of our company which could, in any manner, prejudice our cause, and there was hope yet that we should be able to return to our homes, if for nothing else, at least to find out the guilty man or woman who betrayed us.

To this end we all denied that we had been guilty of intended flight. Master Thomas said that the evidence he had of our intention to run away was strong enough to hang us in a case of murder. "But," said I, "the cases are not equal; if murder were committed,—the thing is done! but we have not run away. Where is the evidence against us? We were quietly at our work." I talked thus with unusual freedom, in order to bring out the evidence against us, for we all wanted, above all things, to know who had betrayed us, that we might have something tangible on which to pour our execrations. From something which dropped, in the course of the talk, it appeared that there was but one witness against us, and that that witness could not be produced. Master Thomas would not tell us who his informant was, but we suspected, and suspected *one* person only. Several circumstances seemed to point Sandy out as our betrayer. His entire knowledge of our plans, his participation in them, his withdrawal from us, his dream and his simultaneous presentiment that we were betrayed, the taking us and the leaving him, were calculated to turn suspicion toward him, and yet we could not suspect him. We all loved him too well to think it possible that he could have betrayed us. So we rolled the guilt on other shoulders.

We were literally dragged, that morning, behind horses, a distance of fifteen miles, and placed in the Easton jail. We were glad to reach the end of our journey, for our pathway had been full of insult and mortification. Such is the power of public opinion, that it is hard, even for the innocent, to feel the happy consolation of innocence when they fall under the maledictions of this power. How could we regard ourselves as in the right, when all about us denounced us as criminals, and had the power and the disposition to treat us as such.

A Flock of Buzzards

In jail we were placed under the care of Mr. Joseph Graham, the sheriff of the county. Henry and John and myself were placed in one room, and Henry Bailey and Charles Roberts in another by themselves. This separation was intended to deprive us of the advantage of concert, and to prevent trouble in jail.

Once shut up, a new set of tormentors came upon us. A swarm of imps in human shape—the slave-traders and agents of slave-traders—who gathered in every country town of the State watching for chances to buy human flesh (as buzzards watch for carrion), flocked in upon us to ascertain if our masters had placed us in jail to be sold. Such a set of debased and villainous creatures I never saw before and hope never to see again. I felt as if surrounded by a pack of *fiends* fresh from *perdition*. They laughed, leered, and grinned at us, saying, "Ah, boys, we have got you, haven't we? So you were going to make your escape? Where were you going to?" After taunting us in this way as long as they liked, they one by one subjected us to an examination, with a view to ascertain our value, feeling our arms and legs and shaking us by the shoulders, to see if we were sound and healthy, impudently asking us, "how we would like to have them for masters?" To such questions we were quite dumb (much to their annoyance). One fellow told me, "if he had me he would cut the devil out of me pretty quick."

These negro-buyers were very offensive to the genteel southern Christian public. They were looked upon in respectable Maryland society as necessary but detestable characters. As a class, they were hardened ruffians, made such by nature and by occupation. Yes, they were the legitimate fruit of slavery, and were second in villainy only to the slaveholders themselves who made such a class *possible.* They were mere hucksters of the slave produce of Maryland and Virginia—coarse, cruel, and swaggering bullies, whose very breathing was of blasphemy and blood.

Prison Conditions

Aside from these slave-buyers who infested the prison from time to time, our quarters were much more comfortable than we had any right to expect them to be. Our allowance of food was small and coarse, but our room was the best in the jail—neat and spacious, and with nothing about it necessarily reminding us of being in prison but its heavy locks and bolts and the black iron lattice-work at the windows. We were prisoners of state compared with most slaves who were put into that Easton jail. But the place was not one of contentment. Bolts, bars, and grated windows are not acceptable to freedom-loving people of any color. The suspense, too, was painful. Every step on the stairway was listened to, in the hope that the comer would cast a ray of light on our fate. We would have given the hair of our heads for half a dozen words with one of the waiters in [local businessman] Sol. Lowe's hotel. Such waiters were in the way of hearing, at the table, the probable course of things. We could see them flitting about in their white jackets in front of this hotel, but could speak to none of them.

Soon after the holidays were over, contrary to all our expectations, Messrs. Hamilton and Freeland came up to Easton; not to make a bargain with "Georgia traders," nor to send us up to Austin Woldfolk, as was usual in the case of runaway-slaves, but to release, from prison, Charles, Henry Harris, Henry Bailey and John Harris, and this, too, without the infliction of a single blow. I was left alone in prison. The innocent had been taken and the guilty left. My friends were separated from me, and apparently forever. This circumstance caused me more pain than any other incident connected with our capture and imprisonment. Thirty-nine lashes on my naked and bleeding back would have been joyfully borne, in preference to this separation from these, the friends of my youth. And yet I could not but feel that I was the victim of something like justice. Why should these young men, who were led into this scheme by me, suffer as much as the instigator? I felt glad that they were released from prison, and from the dread prospect of a life (or death I should rather say) in the rice-swamps. It is due to the noble Henry to say that he was almost as reluctant to leave the prison with me in it as he had been to be tied and dragged to prison. But he and we all knew that we should, in all the likelihoods of the case, be separated, in the event of being sold; and since we were completely in the hands of our owners they concluded it would be best to go peaceably home.

Not until this last separation, dear reader, had I touched those profounder depths of desolation which it is the lot of slaves often to reach. I was solitary and alone within the walls of a stone prison, left to a fate of life-long misery. I had hoped and expected much, for months before, but my hopes and expectations were now withered and blasted. The everdreaded slave life in Georgia, Louisiana, and Alabama—from which escape was next to impossible—now in my loneliness stared me in the face. The possibility of ever becoming anything but an abject slave, a mere machine in the hands of an owner, had now fled, and it seemed to me it had fled forever. A life of living death, beset with the innumerable horrors of the cotton-field and the sugar-plantation, seemed to be my doom. The fiends who rushed into the prison when we were first put there continued to visit me and ply me with questions and tantalizing remarks. I was insulted, but helpless; keenly alive to the demands of justice and liberty, but with no means of asserting them. To talk to those imps about justice or mercy would have been as absurd as to reason with bears and tigers. Lead and steel were the only arguments that they were capable of appreciating, as the events of the subsequent years have proved.

A Beam of Hope

After remaining in this life of misery and despair about a week, which seemed a month, Master Thomas, very much to my surprise and greatly to my relief, came to the prison and took me out, for the purpose, as he said, of sending me to Alabama with a friend of his, who would emancipate me at the end of eight years. I was glad enough to get out of prison, but I had no faith in the story that his friend would emancipate me. Besides, I had never heard of his having a friend in Alabama, and I took the announcement simply as an easy and comfortable method of shipping me off to the far south. There was a little scandal, too, connected with the idea of one Christian selling another to Georgia traders, while it was deemed every way proper for them to sell to others. I thought this friend in Alabama was an invention to meet this difficulty, for Master Thomas was quite jealous of his religious reputation, however unconcerned he might have been about his real Christian character. In these remarks it is possible I do him injustice. He certainly did not exert his power over me as in the case he might have done, but acted, upon the whole, very generously, considering the nature of my offense. He had the power and the provocation to send me, without reserve, into the very Everglades of Florida, beyond the remotest hope of emancipation; and his refusal to exercise that power must be set down to his credit.

After lingering about St. Michaels a few days, and no friend from Alabama appearing, Master Thomas decided to send me back again to Baltimore, to live with his brother Hugh, with whom he was now at peace. Possibly he became so by his profession of religion at the camp-meeting in the Bay-side. Master Thomas told me that he wished me to go to Baltimore and learn a trade; and that if I behaved myself properly he would *emancipate me at twenty five* [i.e., in about five years]. Thanks for this one beam of hope in the future! The promise had but one fault—it seemed too good to be true.

Chapter 5

The Abolition Debate

Chapter Preface

The slave trade between Africa and North America took place during a time when unequal social relations were the norm throughout Europe. The enslavement of human beings came naturally to a people accustomed to living with mastery and servitude. The British aristocrats who made up the first plantation society in America were accustomed to thinking of their own lower classes as brutish, unruly, and fit only for manual labor. Africans, in the opinion of many, were naturally slaves, and very few voices were raised against slavery in the colonies.

Nevertheless, abolitionists were speaking and writing as early as the late seventeenth century. The most eloquent of them came from among religious leaders such as the Quakers in Pennsylvania and the Puritan judge Samuel Sewall in Massachusetts. These voices strengthened in the wake of the American Revolution. The abolitionists insisted on a literal interpretation of the Declaration of Independence and the Constitution, the founding documents of the United States, and on freedom for all people, including slaves. No matter how long and loud the abolitionists spoke out, however, the actual process of emancipation brought them up short. How could emancipated slaves adapt to life among white citizens? What would be the result of this mixing of the races, seen as unnatural by so many? How would slave owners be compensated for the loss of their property? There was little agreement on any of these questions.

The South offered a strong reaction to the abolitionist movement, and Southern writers spent much of their ink explaining slavery as a natural institution in which both blacks and whites benefited. There were faults in the North as well, they pointed out, and evils existed in the labor practices of Northern factories that equaled the worst of what slavery had

to offer. The arguments often grew bitter and personal because the two sides were really arguing over the origins and
true meaning of an experiment still in progress: the United
States. Both sides viewed the issue of slavery as central to
the future of the country, and both eventually reached the
conclusion that the debate could only be resolved by war.

Slavery Brings Economic Prosperity

David Christy

Cincinnati journalist David Christy was neither a southerner, a slaveowner, nor a secessionist. Yet his argument for slavery drew on the South's motto that "Cotton is King"—a position to be seriously reckoned with by northern abolitionists and antislavery legislators. Slavery was the cornerstone of the cotton business, and cotton made up more than half the nation's foreign exports in the decades before the Civil War. Slavery bound the North, South, and Europe together in a powerful economic web, one that many believed could only be disrupted at great danger to the nation's expansion and prosperity.

Christy's book *Cotton Is King* was first published in 1855 and went through three popular editions by the beginning of the Civil War. Southerners pointed to it as a well-reasoned and irrefutable justification of slavery. At the same time, Europe's dependence on southern cotton was assuring cotton planters and secessionists that, eventually, Europe would support their cause and ally with the South if war came—a hope that would not be realized.

T he institution of Slavery, at this moment, gives indications of a vitality that was never anticipated by its friends or foes. Its enemies often supposed it about ready to expire, from the wounds they had inflicted, when in truth it had taken two steps in advance; while they had taken twice

From David Christy, *Cotton Is King* (Cincinnati: Moore, Wilstach, Keys & Co., 1855).

the number in an opposite direction. In each successive conflict, its assailants have been weakened, while its dominion has been extended.

This has arisen from causes too generally overlooked. Slavery is not an isolated system, but is so mingled with the business of the world, that it derives facilities from the most innocent transactions. Capital and labor, in Europe and America, are largely employed in the manufacture of cotton. These goods, to a great extent, may be seen freighting every vessel, from Christian nations, that traverses the seas of the globe; and filling the warehouses and shelves of the merchants, over two-thirds of the world. By the industry, skill, and enterprise, employed in the manufacture of cotton, mankind are better clothed; their comfort better promoted; general industry more highly stimulated; commerce more widely extended; and civilization more rapidly advanced, than in any preceding age.

To the superficial observer, all the agencies, based upon the manufacture and sale of cotton, seem to be legitimately engaged in promoting human happiness; and he, doubtless, feels like invoking Heaven's choicest blessings upon them. When he sees the stockholders in the cotton corporations receiving their dividends, the operatives their wages, the merchants their profits, and civilized people everywhere clothed comfortably in cottons, he can not refrain from explaining: "The lines have fallen unto them in pleasant places; yea, they have a goodly heritage!"

But turn a moment to the source whence the raw cotton, the basis of these operations, is obtained, and observe the aspect of things in that direction. When the statistics on the subject are examined, it appears that nearly all the cotton consumed in the Christian world, is the product of the Slave labor of the United States. It is this monopoly that has given Slavery its commercial value; and, while this monopoly is retained, the institution will continue to extend itself wherever it can find room to spread. He who looks for any other result, must expect that nations, which, for centuries, have waged war to extend their commerce, will now abandon their means of aggrandizement, and bankrupt themselves, to force the abolition of American Slavery!

Commercial Advantages

This is not all. The economical value of Slavery as an agency for supplying the means of extending manufactures and commerce, has long been understood by statesmen. The discovery of the power of steam, and the inventions in machinery, for preparing and manufacturing cotton, revealed the important fact, that a single Island, having the monopoly secured to itself, could supply the world with clothing. *Great Britain attempted to gain this monopoly;* and, to prevent other countries from rivaling her, she long prohibited all emigration of skillful mechanics from the kingdom, as well as all exports of machinery. As country after country was opened to her commerce, the markets for her manufactures were extended, and the demand for the raw material increased. The benefits of this enlarged commerce of the world were not confined to a single nation, but mutually enjoyed by all. As each had products to sell, peculiar to itself, the advantages often gained by one, were no detriment to the others. The principal articles demanded by this increasing commerce, have been coffee, sugar, and cotton—in the production of which Slave labor has greatly predominated. Since the enlargement of manufactures, cotton has entered more extensively into commerce than coffee and sugar, though the demand for all three has advanced with the greatest rapidity. England could only become a great commercial nation, through the agency of her manufactures. She was the best supplied, of all the nations, with the necessary capital, skill, labor, and fuel, to extend her commerce by this means. But, for the raw material, to supply her manufactories, she was dependent upon other countries. The planters of the United States were the most favorably situated for the cultivation of cotton, and attempted *to monopolize the markets for that staple.* This led to a fusion of interests between them and the manufacturers of Great Britain; and to the invention of notions, in political economy, that would, so far as adopted, promote the interests of this coalition. With the advantages possessed by the English manufacturers, "Free Trade" would render all other nations subservient to their interests; and, so far as their operations should be increased, just so far would the demand for American cotton be extended. The details of the success of the parties to this combination, and the opposition they have had to encounter, are left to be noticed more fully hereafter. To the cotton planters, the co-partnership has been eminently advantageous.

Slavery Brings Prosperity

How far the other agricultural interests of the United States are promoted, by extending the cultivation of cotton, may be inferred from the Census returns of 1850, and the Congressional Reports on Commerce and Navigation, for 1854. Cotton and tobacco, only, are largely exported. The production of sugar does not yet equal our consumption of the article, and we import, chiefly from Slave-labor countries, 445,445,680 lbs. to make up the deficiency. But of cotton and tobacco, we export more than *two-thirds* of the amount produced; while of other products, of the agriculturists, less than the *one-forty-sixth* part is exported. Foreign nations, generally, can grow their provisions, but can not grow their tobacco and cotton. Our surplus provisions, not exported, go to the villages, towns, and cities, to feed the mechanics, manufacturers, merchants, professional men, and others; or to the cotton and sugar districts of the South, to feed the planters and their slaves. The increase of mechanics and manufacturers at the North, and the expansion of Slavery at the South, therefore, augment the markets for provisions, and promote the prosperity of the farmer. As the mechanical population increases, the implements of husbandry, and articles of furniture, are multiplied, so that both farmer and planter can be supplied with them on easier terms. As foreign nations open their markets to cotton fabrics, increased demands, for the raw material, are made. As new grazing and grain-growing States are developed, and teem with their surplus productions, the mechanic is benefited, and the planter, relieved from food-raising, can employ his slaves more extensively upon cotton. It is thus that our exports are increased; our foreign commerce advanced; the home markets of the mechanic and farmer extended, and the wealth of the nation promoted. It is thus, also, that the Free labor of the country finds remunerating markets for its products—though at the expense of serving as an efficient auxiliary in the extension of Slavery!

But more. So speedily are new grain-growing States springing up; so vast is the territory owned by the United States, ready for settlement; and so enormous will soon be the amount of products demanding profitable markets, that the national government has been seeking new outlets for them, upon our own continent, to which, alone, they can be advantageously transported. That such outlets, when our vast possessions, Westward, are brought under cultivation, will be an imperious necessity, is known to every statesman. The farmers of these new States, after the example of those of the older sections of the country, will demand a market for their products. This can be furnished, only, by the extension of Slavery; by the acquisition of more tropical territory; by opening the ports of Brazil, and other South American countries, to the admission of our provisions; or by a vast enlargement of domestic manufactures, to the exclusion of foreign goods from the country. Look at this question as it now stands, and then judge of what it must be twenty years hence. The class of products under consideration, in the whole country, in 1853, were valued at $1,551,176,490; of which there were exported to foreign countries, to the value of only $33,809,126. The planter will not assent to any check upon the foreign imports of the country, for the benefit of the farmer. This demands the adoption of vigorous measures to secure a market for his products by some of the other modes stated. Hence, the orders of our Executive, in 1851, for the exploration of the valley of the Amazon; the efforts, in 1854, to obtain a treaty with Brazil for the free navigation of that immense river; the negotiations for a military foothold in St. Domingo, and the determination to acquire Cuba. . . .

The Time Has Not Yet Come

In concluding our labors, there is little need of extended observation. The work of Emancipation, in our country, was
checked, and the extension of Slavery promoted:—first, by
the Free Colored People neglecting to improve the advantages afforded them; second, by the increasing values imparted to Slave-labor; third, by the mistaken policy into
which the Abolitionists have fallen. Whatever reasons might
now be offered, for emancipation, from an improvement of
our Free colored people, is far more than counterbalanced
by its failure in the West Indies, and the constantly increasing value of the labor of the Slave. If, when the Planters had
only a moiety [half] of the markets for Cotton, the value of
Slavery was such as to arrest emancipation, how must the
obstacles be increased, now, when they have the monopoly
of the markets of the world?

We propose not to speak of remedies for Slavery. That we
leave to others. Thus far this great civil and social evil, has
baffled all human wisdom. Either some radical defect must
have existed, in the measures devised for its removal, or the
time has not yet come for successfully assailing the Institution. Our work is completed, in the delineation we have giv-
en of its varied relations to our commercial and social interests. As the monopoly of the culture of Cotton, imparts
to Slavery its economical value, the system will continue as
long as this monopoly is maintained. Slave-Labor products
have now become necessities of human life, to the extent of
more than half the commercial articles supplied to the Christian world. Even Free labor, itself, is made largely subservient to Slavery, and vitally interested in its perpetuation
and extension.

King Cotton's Nature

Can this condition of things be changed? It may be reason-
ably doubted, whether anything efficient can be speedily accomplished: not because there is lack of territory where
freemen may be employed in tropical cultivation; not because intelligent free-labor is less productive than slave-

labor; but because freemen, whose constitutions are adapted to tropical climates, will not avail themselves of the opportunity offered for commencing such an enterprise.

King Cotton cares not whether he employs slaves or freemen. It is the *cotton*, not the *slaves*, upon which his throne is based. Let freemen do his work as well, and he will not object to the change. Thus far the experiments in this respect have failed, and they will not soon be renewed. The efforts of his most powerful ally, Great Britain, to promote that object, have already cost her people many hundreds of millions of dollars: with total failure as a reward for her zeal. One-sixth of the colored people of the United States are

Southern Principles

As outright civil war erupted over the issues of states' rights and slavery, the South's defenders grew more certain of the rightness of their cause and more caustic in their criticism of the North. On May 28, 1863, in the year that proved to be the turning point of the Civil War, the Richmond Examiner *summed up the Southern position.*

The establishment of the Confederacy is, verily, a distinct reaction against the whole course of the mistaken civilization of the age. . . . For 'Liberty, Equality, Fraternity,' we have deliberately substituted Slavery, Subordination, and Government. That there are slave races born to serve, master races born to govern, such are the fundamental principles which we inherit from the ancient world, which are lifted up in the faces of a perverse generation that has forgotten the wisdom of its fathers; by those principles we live, and in their defence we have shown ourselves ready to die. Reverently we feel that our Confederacy is a God-sent missionary to the nations, with great truths to preach. We must speak them boldly, and whoso has ears to hear, let him hear.

free; *but they shun the cotton regions,* and have been instructed to detest *emigration to Liberia.* Their improvement has not been such as was anticipated; and their more rapid advancement cannot be expected, while they remain in the country. The free colored people of the West Indies, can no longer be relied on to furnish tropical products, for they are fast sinking into savage indolence. His Majesty, King Cotton, therefore, is forced to continue the employment of his slaves; and, by their toil, is riding on, conquering and to conquer! He receives no check from the cries of the oppressed, while the citizens of the world are dragging forward his chariot, and shouting aloud his praise!

Abolitionist Problems

King Cotton is a profound statesman, and knows what measures will best sustain his throne. He is an acute mental philosopher, acquainted with the secret springs of human action, and accurately perceives who will best promote his aims. He has no evidence that colored men can grow his cotton, but in the capacity of slaves. It is his policy, therefore, to defeat all schemes of emancipation. To do this, he stirs up such agitations as lure his enemies into measures that will do him no injury. The venal politician is always at his call, and assumes the form of saint or sinner, as the service may demand. Nor does he overlook the enthusiast, engaged in Quixotic endeavors for the relief of suffering humanity, but influences him to advocate measures which tend to tighten, instead of loosing the bands of Slavery. Or, if he cannot be seduced into the support of such schemes, he is beguiled into efforts that waste his strength on objects the most impracticable—so that Slavery receives no damage from the exuberance of his philanthropy. But should such a one, perceiving the futility of his labors, and the evils of his course, make an attempt to avert the consequences; while he is doing this, some new recruit, pushed forward into his former place, charges him with lukewarmness, or Pro-slavery sentiments, destroys his influence with the public, keeps alive the delusions, and sustains the supremacy of King Cotton in the world.

In speaking of the economical connections of Slavery with the other material interests of the world, we have called it a *tri-partite alliance.* It is more than this. It is *quadruple.* Its structure includes four parties, arranged thus: The Western Agriculturists; the Southern Planters; the English Manufacturers; and the American Abolitionists! By this arrangement, the Abolitionists do not stand in direct contact with Slavery:—they imagine, therefore, that they have clean hands and pure hearts, so far as sustaining the system is concerned. But they, no less than their allies, aid in promoting the interests of Slavery. Their sympathies are with England on the Slavery question, and they very naturally incline to agree with her on other points. She advocates *Free Trade,* as essential to her manufactures and commerce; and they do the same, not waiting to inquire into its bearings upon *American Slavery.* We refer now to the people, not to their leaders, whose integrity we choose not to indorse. The Free Trade and Protective Systems, in their bearings upon Slavery, are so well understood, that no man of general reading, especially an editor, who professes Anti-Slavery sentiments, at the same time advocating Free Trade, will ever convince men of intelligence, pretend what he may, that he is not either woefully perverted in his judgment, or emphatically, a "dough-face" in disguise! England, we were about to say, is in alliance with the cotton planter, to whose prosperity Free Trade is indispensable. Abolitionism is in alliance with England. All three of these parties, then, agree in their support of the Free Trade policy. It needed but the aid of the Western Farmer, therefore, to give permanency to this principle. His adhesion has been given, the *quadruple alliance* has been perfected, and Slavery and Free Trade *nationalized*!

The crisis now upon the country, as a consequence of Slavery having become dominant, demands that the highest wisdom should be brought to the management of national affairs. The *quacks* who have aided in producing the malady, and who have the effrontery still to claim the right to manage the case, must be dismissed. The men who mock at the Political Economy of the North, and have assisted in crushing its cherished policy, must be rebuked. Slavery, *nationalized,* can now be managed only as a national concern. It can now be abolished only with the consent of those who sustain it. Their assent can be gained only on employing other agents to meet the wants it now supplies. It must be superseded, then, if at all, by means that will not injuriously affect the interests of commerce and agriculture, to which it is now so important an auxiliary. To supply the demand for tropical products, except by the present mode, is not the work of a day, nor of a generation. Should the influx of foreigners continue, such a change may be possible. But to effect the transition from Slavery to Freedom, on principles that will be acceptable to the parties who control the question; to devise and successfully sustain such measures as will produce this result; must be left to statesmen of broader views and loftier conceptions than are to be found among those at present engaged in this great controversy.

Northern Slavery

George Fitzhugh

> An outspoken champion of slavery, George Fitzhugh justified
> his position with a scathing attack on what he called "white
> slavery," or the exploitation of wage laborers by wealthy
> northern capitalists. To Fitzhugh's way of thinking, black
> slaves enjoyed a far better way of life than "white slaves,"
> who suffered neglect and oppression at the hands of the mon-
> eyed classes that benefited from their endless toil. It was an
> argument drawing, somewhat perversely, on the socialist the-
> ories of Karl Marx and Friedrich Engels that would gain
> strength among the workers of the industrial world in the lat-
> ter half of the nineteenth century. To Fitzhugh, laissez-faire
> capitalism was the world's true economic evil, and slavery the
> most natural and happy condition for the African and his
> descendants in America.

We are all, North and South, engaged in the White Slave
Trade, and he who succeeds best is esteemed most respectable. It is far more cruel than the Black Slave Trade,
because it exacts more of its slaves, and neither protects nor
governs them. We boast that it exacts more when we say,
"that the *profits* made from employing free labor are greater
than those from slave labor." The profits, made from free labor, are the amount of the products of such labor, which the
employer, by means of the command which capital or skill
gives him, takes away, exacts, or "exploitates" [exploits]
from the free laborer. The profits of slave labor are that portion of the products of such labor which the power of the

From George Fitzhugh, *Cannibals All! or, Slaves Without Masters* (Richmond, VA:
A. Morris, 1857).

master enables him to appropriate. These profits are less, because the master allows the slave to retain a larger share of the results of his own labor than do the employers of free labor. But we not only boast that the White Slave Trade is more exacting and fraudulent (in fact, though not in intention) than Black Slavery; but we also boast that it is more cruel, in leaving the laborer to take care of himself and family out of the pittance which skill or capital have allowed him to retain. When the day's labor is ended, he is free, but is overburdened with the cares of family and household, which make his freedom an empty and delusive mockery. But his employer is really free, and may enjoy the profits made by others' labor, without a care, or a trouble, as to their well-being. The negro slave is free, too, when the labors of the day are over, and free in mind as well as body; for the master provides food, raiment, house, fuel, and everything else necessary to the physical well-being of himself and family. The master's labors commence just when the slave's end. No wonder men should prefer white slavery to capital, to negro slavery, since it is more profitable, and is free from all the cares and labors of black slave-holding.

The Four Classes

Now, reader, if you wish to know yourself—to "descant on your own deformity"—read on. But if you would cherish self-conceit, self-esteem, or self-appreciation, throw down our book; for we will dispel illusions which have promoted your happiness, and show you that what you have considered and practiced as virtue is little better than moral Cannibalism. But you will find yourself in numerous and respectable company; for all good and respectable people are "Cannibals all" who do not labor, or who are successfully trying to live without labor, on the unrequited labor of other people:—Whilst low, bad, and disreputable people, are those who labor to support themselves, and to support said respectable people besides. Throwing the negro slaves out of the account, and society is divided in Christendom into four classes: the rich, or independent respectable people, who live well and labor not at all, the professional and skillful respectable people, who do a little light work, for enormous wages; the poor hard-working people, who support everybody, and starve themselves; and the poor thieves, swindlers, and sturdy beggars, who live like gentlemen, without labor, on the labor of other people. The gentlemen exploitate, which being done on a large scale and requiring a great many victims, is highly respectable—whilst the rogues and beggars take so little from others that they fare little better than those who labor.

But, reader, we do not wish to fire into the flock. "Thou art the man!" You are a Cannibal! and if a successful one, pride yourself on the number of your victims quite as much as any Fiji chieftain, who breakfasts, dines, and sups on human flesh—and your conscience smites you, if you have failed to succeed, quite as much as his, when he returns from an unsuccessful foray.

The Native of Labor

Probably, you are a lawyer, or a merchant, or a doctor, who has made by your business fifty thousand dollars, and retired to live on your capital. But, mark! not to spend your capital. That would be vulgar, disreputable, criminal. That would be, to live by your own labor; for your capital is your amassed labor. That would be to do as common working men do; for they take the pittance which their employers leave them to live on. They live by labor; for they exchange the results of their own labor for the products of other people's labor. It is, no doubt, an honest, vulgar way of living, but not at all a respectable way. The respectable way of living is to make other people work for you, and to pay them nothing for so doing—and to have no concern about them after their work is done. Hence, white slave-holding is much more respectable than negro slavery—for the master works nearly as hard for the negro as he for the master. But you, my virtuous, respectable reader, exact three thousand dollars per annum. from white labor (for your income is the product of white labor) and make not one cent of return in any form. You retain your capital, and never labor, and yet live in luxury on the labor of others. Capital commands labor, as the master does the slave. Neither pays for labor; but the master permits the slave to retain a larger allowance from the proceeds of his own labor, and hence "free labor is cheaper than slave labor." You, with the command over labor which your capital gives you, are a slave owner—a master, without the obligations of a master. They who work for you, who create your income, are slaves, without the rights of slaves. Slaves without a master! Whilst you were engaged in amassing your capital, in seeking to become independent, you were in the White Slave Trade. To become independent is to be able to make other people support you, without being obliged to labor for *them*. Now, what man in society is not seeking to attain this situation? He who attains it is a slave owner, in the worst sense. He who is in pursuit of it is engaged in the slave trade. You, reader, belong to the one or other class. The men without property, in free society, are theoretically in a worse condition than slaves. Practically, their condition corresponds with this theory, as history and statistics everywhere demonstrate. The capitalists, in free society, live in ten times the luxury and show [than] Southern masters do, because the slaves to capital work harder and cost less than negro slaves.

The Joys of Slavery

The negro slaves of the South are the happiest, and, in some sense, the freest people in the world. The children and the aged and infirm work not at all, and yet have all the comforts and necessaries of life provided for them. They enjoy liberty, because they are oppressed neither by care nor labor. The women do little hard work, and are protected from the despotism of their husbands by their masters. The negro men and stout boys work, on the average, in good weather, not more than nine hours a day. The balance of their time is spent in perfect abandon. Besides, they have their Sabbaths and holidays. White men, with so much of license and liberty, would die of ennui; but negroes luxuriate in corporeal [physical] and mental repose. With their faces upturned to the sun, they can sleep at any hour; and quiet sleep is the greatest of human enjoyments. "Blessed be the man who invented sleep." 'Tis happiness in itself—and results from contentment with the present, and confident assurance of the future. We do not know whether free laborers ever sleep. They are fools to do so; for, whilst they sleep, the wily and watchful capitalist is devising means to ensnare and exploitate them. The free laborer must work or starve. He is more of a slave than the negro, because he works longer and harder for less allowance than the slave, and has no holiday, because the cares of life with him begin when its labors end. He has no liberty, and not a single right. We know, 'tis often said, air and water are common property, which all have equal right to participate and enjoy; but this is utterly false. The appropriation of the lands carries with it the appropriation of all on or above the lands, *usque ad coelum, aut ad inferos* ["even to heaven or to hell"]. A man cannot breathe the air without a place to breathe it from, and all places are appropriated. All water is private property "to the middle of the stream," except the ocean, and that is not fit to drink.

Free laborers have not a thousandth part of the rights and liberties of negro slaves. Indeed, they have not a single liberty, unless it be the right or liberty to die. But the reader may think that he and other capitalists and employers are freer than negro slaves. Your capital would soon vanish, if you dared indulge in the liberty and abandon of negroes. You hold your wealth and position by the tenure of constant watchfulness, care, and circumspection. You never labor; but you are never free.

Where a few own the soil, they have unlimited power over the balance of society, until domestic slavery comes in to compel them to permit this balance of society to draw a sufficient and comfortable living from *terra mater* ["mother earth"]. Free society asserts the right of a few to the earth—slavery maintains that it belongs, in different degrees, to all.

Capitalism Is Slavery

But, reader, well may you follow the slave trade. It is the only trade worth following, and slaves the only property worth owning. All other is worthless, a mere *caput mortuum* ["worthless residue"], except in so far as it vests the owner with the power to command the labors of others—to enslave them. Give you a palace, ten thousand acres of land, sumptuous clothes, equipage, and every other luxury; and with your artificial wants you are poorer than Robinson Crusoe, or the lowest working man, if you have no slaves to capital, or domestic slaves. Your capital will not bring you an income of a cent, nor supply one of your wants, without labor. Labor is indispensable to give value to property, and if you owned every thing else, and did not own labor, you would be poor. But fifty thousand dollars means, and is, fifty thousand dollars worth of slaves. You can command, without touching on that capital, three thousand dollars' worth of labor per annum. You could do no more were you to buy slaves with it, and then you would be cumbered with the cares of governing and providing for them. You are a slaveholder now, to the amount of fifty thousand dollars, with all the advantages, and none of the cares and responsibilities of a [slave] master.

"Property in man" is what all are struggling to obtain. Why should they not be obliged to take care of man, their property, as they do of their horses and their hounds, their cattle and their sheep. Now, under the delusive name of liberty, you work him "from morn to dewy eve"—from infancy to old age—then turn him out to starve. You treat your horses and hounds better. Capital is a cruel master. The free slave trade, the commonest, yet the cruellest of trades.

Proclaiming the Abolitionist Creed

William Lloyd Garrison

William Lloyd Garrison of Massachusetts was a man of causes: temperance, women's rights, pacifism, and the protection of Native Americans. But he fought longest and loudest for the abolition of slavery, long before abolition was fashionable. Garrison's journal, *The Liberator,* remained the best known abolitionist publication in the country, and Garrison brought it out faithfully from 1831 until the end of the Civil War. In his editorials and speeches, Garrison never compromised his belief that slavery was a great wrong that should be abolished at any cost, even the cost of outright warfare with the slaveowning interests of the South. His beliefs led Garrison to denounce the Constitution, renounce his allegiance to the United States, and at one point propose the secession of an entire region of the country—the North.

In urging the complete and immediate abolition of slavery, Garrison often found himself dangerously ahead of his time. In 1825, at the tender age of twenty and still six years before bringing out the first edition of *The Liberator,* he made the following statement of his principles. The speech drew an angry response throughout the northern United States, where people may have abhorred slavery but had no notion of ever seeing it abolished—especially not at the cost of strife among the states.

From Wendell Phillips Garrison and Francis Jackson Garrison, *William Lloyd Garrison, 1805–1879: The Story of His Life Told by His Children* (New York: Century, 1885–1889).

Sirs, I am not come to tell you that slavery is a curse, debasing in its effect, cruel in its operation, fatal in its continuance. The day and the occasion require no such revelation. I do not claim the discovery as my own, that "all men are born equal," and that among their inalienable rights are "life, liberty, and the pursuit of happiness." Were I addressing any other than a free and Christian assembly, the enforcement of this truth might be pertinent. Neither do I intend to analyze the horrors of slavery for your inspection, nor to freeze your blood with authentic recitals of savage cruelty. Nor will time allow me to explore even a furlong of that immense wilderness of suffering which remains unsubdued in our land. I take it for granted that the existence of these evils is acknowledged, if not rightly understood. My object is to define and enforce our duty, as Christians and Philanthropists.

Four Points on Slavery

On a subject so exhaustless, it will be impossible, in the moiety [half] of an address, to unfold all the facts which are necessary to its full development. In view of it, my heart swells up like a living fountain, which time cannot exhaust, for it is perpetual. Let this be considered as a preface of a noble work, which your inventive sympathies must elaborate and complete.

I assume as distinct and defensible propositions,

I. That the slaves of this country, whether we consider their moral, intellectual or social condition, are preëminently entitled to the prayers, and sympathies, and charities, of the American people; and their claims for redress are as strong as those of any Americans could be in a similar condition.

II. That, as the free States—by which I mean non-slaveholding States—are constitutionally involved in the guilt of slavery, by adhering to a national compact that sanctions it; and in the danger, by liability to be called upon for aid in case of insurrection; they have the right to remonstrate against its continuance, and it is their duty to assist in its overthrow.

III. That no justificative plea for the perpetuity of slavery can be found in the condition of its victims; and no barrier against our righteous interference, in the laws which authorize the buying, selling and possessing of slaves, nor in the hazard of a collision with slaveholders.

IV. That education and freedom will elevate our colored population to a rank with the white—making them useful, intelligent and peaceable citizens.

In the first place, it will be readily admitted, that it is the duty of every nation primarily to administer relief to its own necessities, to cure its own maladies, to instruct its own children, and to watch over its own interests. He is "worse than an infidel" who neglects his own household, and squanders his earnings upon strangers; and the policy of that nation is unwise which seeks to proselyte other portions of the globe at the expense of its safety and happiness. Let me not be misunderstood. My benevolence is neither contracted nor selfish. I pity that man whose heart is not larger than a whole continent. I despise the littleness of that patriotism which blusters only for its own rights, and, stretched to its utmost dimensions, scarcely covers its native territory; which adopts as its creed the right to act independently, even to the verge of licentiousness, without restraint, and to tyrannize wherever it can with impunity. This sort of patriotism is common. I suspect the reality, and deny the productiveness, of that piety which confines its operations to a particular spot—if that spot be less than the whole earth; nor scoops out, in every direction, new channels for the waters of life. Christian charity, while it "begins at home," goes abroad in search of misery. It is as copious as the sun in heaven. It does not, like the Nile, make a partial inundation, and then withdraw; but it perpetually overflows, and fertilizes every barren spot. It is restricted only by the exact number of God's suffering creatures. But I mean to say, that, while we are aiding and instructing foreigners, we ought not to forget our own degraded countrymen; that neither duty nor honesty requires us to defraud ourselves that we may enrich others.

The Slave as Citizen

The condition of the slaves, in a religious point of view, is deplorable, entitling them to a higher consideration, on our part, than any other race; higher than the Turks or Chinese, for they have the privileges of instruction; higher than the Pagans, for they are not dwellers in a gospel land; higher than our red men of the forest, for we do not bind them with gyves [shackles], nor treat them as chattels.

And here let me ask, What has Christianity done, by direct effort, for our slave population? Comparatively nothing. She has explored the isles of the ocean for objects of commiseration; but, amazing stupidity! she can gaze without emotion on a multitude of miserable beings at home, large enough to constitute a nation of freemen, whom tyranny has heathenized by law. In her public services they are seldom remembered, and in her private donations they are forgotten. From one end of the country to the other, her charitable societies form golden links of benevolence, and scatter their contributions like raindrops over a parched heath; but they bring no sustenance to the perishing slave. The blood of souls is upon her garments, yet she heeds not the stain. The clankings of the prisoner's chains strike upon her ear, but they cannot penetrate her heart.

I have said that the claims of the slaves for redress are as strong as those of any Americans could be, in a similar condition. Does any man deny the position? The proof, then, is found in the fact, that a very large proportion of our colored population were born on our soil, and are therefore entitled to all the privileges of American citizens. This is their country by birth, not by adoption. Their children possess the same inherent and unalienable rights as ours, and it is a crime of the blackest dye to load them with fetters.

Every Fourth of July, our Declaration of Independence is produced, with a sublime indignation, to set forth the tyranny of the mother country, and to challenge the admiration of the world. But what a pitiful detail of grievances does this document present, in comparison with the wrongs which our slaves endure! In the one case, it is hardly the plucking of a hair from the head; in the other, it is the crushing of a live body on the wheel—the stings of the wasp contrasted with the tortures of the Inquisition. Before God, I must say, that such a glaring contradiction as exists between our creed and practice the annals of six thousand years cannot parallel. In view of it, I am ashamed of my country. I am sick of our unmeaning declamation in praise of liberty and equality; of our hypocritical cant about the unalienable rights of man. I could not, for my right hand, stand up before a European assembly, and exult that I am an American citizen, and denounce the usurpations of a kingly government as wicked and unjust; or, should I make the attempt, the recollection of my country's barbarity and despotism would blister my lips, and cover my cheeks with burning blushes of shame. . . .

The Difficult Work Ahead

If it be still objected, that it would be dangerous to liberate the present race of blacks:

I answer—the emancipation of all the slaves of this generation is most assuredly out of the question. The fabric, which now towers above the Alps, must be taken away brick by brick, and foot by foot, till it is reduced so low that it may be overturned without burying the nation in its ruins. Years may elapse before the completion of the achievement; generations of blacks may go down to the grave, manacled and lacerated, without a hope for their children; the philanthropists who are now pleading in behalf of the oppressed, may not live to witness the dawn which will precede the glorious day of universal emancipation; but the work will go on—laborers in the cause will multiply—new resources will be discovered—the victory will be obtained, worth the desperate struggle of a thousand years. Or, if defeat follow, woe to the safety of this people! The nation will be shaken as if by a mighty earthquake. A cry of horror, a cry of revenge, will go up to heaven in the darkness of midnight, and re-echo from every cloud. Blood will flow like water—the blood of guilty men, and of innocent women and children. Then will be heard lamentations and weeping, such as will blot out the remembrance of the horrors of St. Domingo [the violent Haitian revolution]. The terrible judgments of an incensed God will complete the catastrophe of republican America.

And since so much is to be done for our country; since so many prejudices are to be dispelled, obstacles vanquished, interests secured, blessings obtained; since the cause of emancipation must progress heavily, and meet with much unhallowed opposition,—why delay the work? There must be a beginning, and now is a propitious time—perhaps the

An Early Abolitionist Expounds

Samuel Sewall of the Massachusetts Colony won public notice for his actions as a judge during the Salem witch trials. But Sewall also wrote New England's first antislavery tract, The Selling of Joseph: A Memorial. *In this passage, which he entitled "Caveat Emptor!" ("Let the Buyer Beware!"), Sewall argues against a biblical justification for slavery and also makes the point that slavery disrupts public order through the mixing of the races.*

All things considered, it would conduce more to the Welfare of the Province, to have White Servants for a Term of Years, than to have Slaves for Life. Few can endure to hear of a Negro's being made free; and indeed they can seldom use their freedom well; yet their continual aspiring after their forbidden Liberty, renders them Unwilling Servants. And there is such a disparity in their Conditions, Colour & Hair, that they can never embody with us, and grow up into orderly Families, to the Peopling of the Land: but still remain in our Body Politick as a kind of extravasat [extruded] Blood. As many Negro men as there are among us, so many empty places there are in our Train Bands [militias], and the places taken up of Men that might make Husbands for our Daughters. And the Sons and Daughters of *New England* would become more like *Jacob*, and last opportunity that will be granted us by a long-suffering God. No temporizing, lukewarm measures will avail aught. We must put our shoulders to the wheel, and heave with our united strength. Let us not look coldly on and see our Southern [anti-slavery] brethren contending single-handed against an all-powerful foe—faint, weary, borne down to the earth. We are all alike guilty. Slavery is strictly a national sin. New-England money has been expended in buying human flesh; New-England ships have been freighted with sable victims; New-England men have assisted in forging the fetters of those who groan in bondage.

Rachel, if this Slavery were thrust quite out of doors. Moreover it is too well known what Temptations Masters are under, to connive at the Fornication of their Slaves; lest they should be obliged to find them Wives, or pay their Fines [for violating colonial statutes such as those against adultery]. It seems to be practically pleaded that they might be Lawless; 'tis thought much of, that the Law should have Satisfaction for their Thefts, and other Immoralities; by which means *Holiness to the Lord,* is more rarely engraven upon this sort of Servitude. It is likewise most lamentable to think, how in taking Negros out of *Africa*, and Selling of them here, That which GOD has joyned together men do boldly rend asunder; Men from their Country, Husbands from their Wives, Parents from their Children. How horrible is the Uncleanness, Mortality, if not Murder, that the Ships are guilty of that bring great [crowds] of these miserable Men, and Women. Methinks, when we are bemoaning the barbarous Usage of our Friends and Kinsfolk in *Africa*: it might not be unseasonable to enquire whether we are not culpable in forcing the *Africans* to become Slaves amongst our selves. And it may be a question whether all the Benefit received by *Negro* Slaves, will balance the Accompt [amount] of Cash laid out upon them; and for the Redemption of our own enslaved Friends out of *Africa*. Besides all the Persons and Estates that have perished there.

A Call to Action

I call upon the ambassadors of Christ everywhere to make known this proclamation: "Thus saith the Lord God of the Africans, Let this people go, that they may serve me." I ask them to "proclaim liberty to the captives, and the opening of the prison to them that are bound"—to light up a flame of philanthropy that shall burn till all Africa be redeemed from the night of moral death, and the song of deliverance be heard throughout her borders.

I call upon the churches of the living God to lead in this great enterprise. If the soul be immortal, priceless, save it from remediless woe. Let them combine their energies, and systematize their plans, for the rescue of suffering humanity. Let them pour out their supplications to heaven in behalf of the slave. Prayer is omnipotent: its breath can melt adamantine rocks—its touch can break the stoutest chains. Let anti-slavery charity-boxes stand uppermost among those for missionary, tract and educational purposes. On this subject, Christians have been asleep; let them shake off their slumbers, and arm for the holy contest.

I call upon our New-England women to form charitable associations to relieve the degraded of their sex. As yet, an appeal to their sympathies was never made in vain. They outstrip us in every benevolent race. Females are doing much for the cause at the South; let their example be imitated, and their exertions surpassed, at the North.

I call upon our citizens to assist in establishing auxiliary colonization [relocation] societies in every State, county and town. I implore their direct and liberal patronage to the parent society.

I call upon the great body of newspaper editors to keep this subject constantly before their readers; to sound the trumpet of alarm, and to plead eloquently for the rights of man. They must give the tone to public sentiment. One press may ignite twenty; a city may warm a State; a State may impart a generous heat to a whole country.

I call upon the American people to enfranchise a spot over

which they hold complete sovereignty; to cleanse that worse than Augean stable, the District of Columbia, from its foul impurities. I ask them to sustain Congress in any future efforts to colonize the colored population of the States. I conjure them to select those as Representatives who are not too ignorant to know, too blind to see, nor too timid to perform their duty.

I will say, finally, that I despair of the republic while slavery exists therein. If I look up to God for success, no smile of mercy or forgiveness dispels the gloom of futurity; if to our own resources, they are daily diminishing; if to all history, our destruction is not only possible, but almost certain. Why should we slumber at this momentous crisis? If our hearts were dead to every throb of humanity; if it were lawful to oppress, where power is ample; still, if we had any regard for our safety and happiness, we should strive to crush the Vampire which is feeding upon our life-blood. All the selfishness of our nature cries aloud for a better security. Our own vices are too strong for us, and keep us in perpetual alarm; how, in addition to these, shall we be able to contend successfully with millions of armed and desperate men, as we must eventually, if slavery do not cease?

Destroying Slavery with the Ballot

Hinton Helper

Published in New York in 1857, *The Impending Crisis of the South* provided some heavy artillery for abolitionist leaders in the North. The only book to directly provoke a Congressional debate over slavery in the United States Congress, it combined skillful use of statistics with powerful rhetoric, inspiring widespread praise as well as bitter denunciation. It was said that no one reading Helper's fiery prose came away neutral in the fight over slavery.

Hinton Rowan Helper had been a complete unknown, a small-time farmer from rural North Carolina who migrated north to publish his book at his own expense. As an antislavery southerner, he attracted the support of Horace Greeley, an influential New York newspaper editor who opposed the extension of legalized slavery to the western states and territories. Helper also found sponsorship from the newly founded Republican party, whose members adopted and promoted the book to win support for their "Free Soil" platform.

In his chapter entitled "How Slavery Can Be Abolished," Helper lays out his plan of attack on the slaveowners and slave hirers of the South. Determining that the number of slaveholders is small in comparison to the entire white population in the South, Helper prompts poor non-slaveholders to democratically eliminate slavery by their majority vote and rid themselves of the evil institution that keeps the rich slaveowners in power.

From Hinton Helper, *The Impending Crisis in the South: How to Meet It* (New York: Burdick Brothers, 1857).

Thus far, in giving expression to our sincere and settled opinions, we have endeavored to show, in the first place, that slavery is a great moral, social, civil, and political evil—a dire enemy to true wealth and national greatness, and an atrocious crime against both God and man; and, in the second place, that it is a paramount duty which we owe to heaven, to the earth, to America, to humanity, to our posterity, to our consciences, and to our pockets, to adopt effectual and judicious measures for its immediate abolition. The questions now arise, How can the evil be averted? What are the most prudent and practical means that can be devised for the abolition of slavery? In the solution of these problems it becomes necessary to deal with a multiplicity of stubborn realities. And yet, we can see no reason why North Carolina, in her sovereign capacity, may not, with equal ease and success, do what forty-five other States of the world have done within the last forty-five years. Nor do we believe any good reason exists why Virginia should not perform as great a deed in 1859 as did New-York in 1799. Massachusetts abolished slavery in 1780; would it not be a masterly stroke of policy in Tennessee, and every other slave State, to abolish it in or before 1860?

An Oppressed Majority

Not long since, a slavocrat, writing on this subject, said, apologetically, "we frankly admit that slavery is a monstrous evil; but what are we to do with an institution which has baffled the wisdom of our greatest statesmen?" Unfortunately for the South, since the days of Washington, Jefferson, Madison, and their illustrious compatriots, she has never had more than half a dozen statesmen, all told; of mere politicians, wire-pullers, and slave-driving demagogues, she has had enough, and to spare; but of statesmen, in the true sense of the term, she has had, and now has, but precious few—fewer just at this time, perhaps, than ever before. It is far from a matter of surprise to us that slavery has, for such a long period, baffled the "wisdom" of the oligarchy; but our surprise is destined to culminate in amazement, if the wisdom of the non-slaveholders does not soon baffle slavery.

From the eleventh year previous to the close of the eighteenth century down to the present moment, slaveholders and slave-breeders, who, to speak naked truth, are, as a general thing, unfit to occupy any honorable station in life, have, by chicanery and usurpation, wielded all the official power of the South; and, excepting the patriotic services of the noble abolitionists above-mentioned, the sole aim and drift of their legislation has been to aggrandize themselves, to strengthen slavery, and to keep the poor whites, the constitutional majority, bowed down in the deepest depths of degradation. We propose to subvert this entire system of oligarchal despotism. We think there should be *some* legislation for decent white men, not alone for negroes and slaveholders. Slavery lies at the root of all the shame, poverty, ignorance, tyranny and imbecility of the South; slavery must be thoroughly eradicated; let this be done, and a glorious future will await us.

Non-Slaveholders Arise!

The statesmen who are to abolish slavery in Kentucky, must be mainly and independently constituted by the non-slaveholders of Kentucky; so in every other slave State. Past experience has taught us the sheer folly of ever expecting voluntary justice from the slaveholders. Their illicit intercourse with "the mother of harlots" has been kept up so long, and their whole natures have, in consequence, become so depraved, that there is scarcely a spark of honor or magnanimity to be found amongst them. As well might one expect to hear highwaymen clamoring for a universal interdict against traveling, as to expect slaveholders to pass laws for the abolition of slavery. Under all the circumstances, it is the duty of the non-slaveholders to mark out an independent course for themselves, to steer entirely clear of the oligarchy, and to utterly contemn [condemn] and ignore the many vile instruments of power, animate and inanimate, which have been so freely and so effectually used for their enslavement. Now is the time for them to assert their rights and liberties; never before was there such an appropriate period to strike for Freedom in the South.

Had it not been for the better sense, the purer patriotism, and the more practical justice of the non-slaveholders, the Middle States and New England would still be groaning and groveling under the ponderous burden of slavery; New-York would never have risen above the dishonorable level of Virginia; Pennsylvania, trampled beneath the iron-heel of the black code, would have remained the unprogressive parallel of Georgia; Massachusetts would have continued till the present time, and Heaven only knows how much longer, the contemptible coequal of South Carolina.

Succeeded by the happiest moral effects and the grandest physical results, we have seen slavery crushed beneath the wisdom of the non-slaveholding statesmen of the North; followed by corresponding influences and achievements, many of us who have not yet passed the meridian of life, are destined to see it equally crushed beneath the wisdom of the non-slaveholding Statesmen of the South. With righteous indignation, we enter our disclaimer against the base yet baseless admission that Louisiana and Texas are incapable of producing as great statesmen as Rhode Island and Connecticut. What has been done for New Jersey by the statesmen of New Jersey, can be done for North Carolina by the statesmen of North Carolina; the wisdom of the former State has abolished slavery; as sure as the earth revolves on its axis, the wisdom of the latter will not do less.

That our plan for the abolition of slavery, is the best that can be devised, we have not the vanity to contend; but that it is a good one, and will do to act upon until a better shall have been suggested, we do firmly and conscientiously believe. Though but little skilled in the delicate art of surgery, we have pretty thoroughly probed slavery, the frightful tumor on the body politic, and have, we think, ascertained the precise remedies requisite for a speedy and perfect cure. Possibly the less ardent friends of freedom may object to our prescription, on the ground that some of its ingredients are too griping, and that it will cost the patient a deal of most excruciating pain. But let them remember that the patient is exceedingly refractory, that the case is a desperate one, and that drastic remedies are indispensably necessary. When they shall have invented milder yet equally efficacious ones, it will be time enough to discontinue the use of ours—then no one will be readier than we to discard the infallible strong recipe for the infallible mild. Not at the persecution of a few thousand slaveholders, but at the restitution of natural rights and prerogatives to several millions of non-slaveholders, do we aim.

The Plan of Action

Inscribed on the banner, which we herewith unfurl to the world, with the full and fixed determination to stand by it or die by it, unless one of more virtuous efficacy shall be presented, are the mottoes which, in substance, embody the principles, as we conceive, that should govern us in our patriotic warfare against the most subtle and insidious foe that ever menaced the inalienable rights and liberties and dearest interests of America:

1st. Thorough Organization and Independent Political Action on the part of the Non-Slaveholding whites of the South.

2nd. Ineligibility of Slaveholders—Never another vote to the Trafficker in Human Flesh.

3rd. No Co-operation with Slaveholders in Politics—No Fellowship with them in Religion—No Affiliation with them in Society.

4th. No Patronage to Slaveholding Merchants—No Guestship in Slave-waiting Hotels—No Fees to Slaveholding Lawyers—No Employment of Slaveholding Physicians—No Audience to Slaveholding Parsons.

5th. No Recognition of Pro-slavery Men, except as Ruffians, Outlaws, and Criminals.

6th. Abrupt Discontinuance of Subscription to Pro-slavery Newspapers.

7th. The Greatest Possible Encouragement to Free White Labor.

8th. No more Hiring of Slaves by Non-slaveholders.

9th. Immediate Death to Slavery, or if not immediate, unqualified Proscription of its Advocates during the Period of its Existence.

10th. A Tax of Sixty Dollars on every Slaveholder for each and every Negro in his Possession at the present time, or at any intermediate time between now and the 4th of July, 1863—said Money to be Applied to the transportation of the Blacks to Liberia, to their Colonization in Central or South America, or to their Comfortable Settlement within the Boundaries of the United States.

11th. An additional Tax of Forty Dollars per annum to be levied annually, on every Slaveholder for each and every Negro found in his possession after the 4th of July, 1863— said Money to be paid into the hands of the Negroes so held in Slavery, or, in cases of death, to their next of kin, and to be used by them at their own option.

This, then, is the Outline of our scheme for the abolition of slavery in the Southern States. Let it be acted upon with due promptitude, and, as certain as truth is mightier than error, fifteen years will not elapse before every foot of territory, from the mouth of the Delaware to the emboguing [mouth] of the Rio Grande, will glitter with the jewels of freedom.

Regaining Power

Some time during this year, next, or the year following, let there be a general convention of non-slaveholders from every slave State in the Union, to deliberate on the momentous issues now pending. First, let them adopt measures for holding in restraint the diabolical excesses of the oligarchy; secondly, in order to cast off the thraldom which the infamous slave-power has fastened upon them, and, as the first step necessary to be taken to regain the inalienable rights and liberties with which they were invested by Nature, but of which they have been divested by the accursed dealers in human flesh, let them devise ways and means for the complete annihilation of slavery; thirdly, let them put forth an equitable and comprehensive platform, fully defining their position, and inviting the active sympathy and co-operation of the millions of down-trodden non-slaveholders throughout the Southern and Southwestern States. Let all these things be done, not too hastily, but with calmness, deliberation, prudence, and circumspection; if need be, let the delegates to the convention continue in session one or two weeks; only let their labors be wisely and thoroughly performed; let them, on Wednesday morning, present to the poor whites of the South, a well-digested scheme for the reclamation of their ancient rights and prerogatives, and, on the Thursday following, slavery in the United States will be worth absolutely less than nothing; for then, besides being so vile and precarious that nobody will want it, it will be a lasting reproach to those in whose hands it is lodged.

Were it not that other phases of the subject admonish us to be economical of space, we could suggest more than a dozen different plans, either of which, if scrupulously carried out, would lead to a wholesome, speedy, and perfect termination of slavery. Under all the circumstances, however, it might be difficult for us—perhaps it would not be the easiest thing in the world for any body else—to suggest a better plan than the one above. Let it, or one embodying its principal features, be adopted forthwith, and the last wail of slavery will soon be heard, growing fainter and fainter, till it dies utterly away, to be succeeded by the jubilant shouts of emancipated millions.

Chronology

1619
The first slaves to work on the North American mainland arrive at the Jamestown, Virginia, colony.

1688
The Quakers of Pennsylvania publish the first antislavery document in North America.

1776
Representatives of the British colonists adopt the Declaration of Independence, which grants "life, liberty, and happiness" as natural rights.

1787
By the Northwest Ordinance, written by Thomas Jefferson of Virginia, slavery is banned in new colonies acquired from Great Britain.

1788
The U.S. Constitution is ratified, allowing for slaveholding states to count slaves as three-fifths of a person when determining congressional representation.

1793
By the passage of the first Fugitive Slave Act, escaped slaves must be returned across state lines to their owners; Eli Whitney invents the cotton gin, an important factor in the growth of Southern cotton plantations dependent on slave labor.

1807
Following the U.S. Constitution, which decreed an end to the transatlantic slave trade after twenty years, Congress passes a law to abolish the slave trade in 1808.

1821
The Missouri Compromise admits Missouri as a slave state, Maine as a free state, and bans slavery in new territories lying north of Missouri's southern border.

1831
Abolitionist William Lloyd Garrison begins publication of the *Liberator*; the Nat Turner Rebellion erupts in southern Virginia, killing fifty-nine whites before being put down; Turner eludes capture for six weeks.

1846–1847
The Wilmot Proviso proposes to ban slavery in any new territory acquired in the Mexican War; the measure is repeatedly passed in the House of Representatives but is defeated in the Senate.

1850
By the Compromise of 1850, California is admitted as a free state; the Fugitive Slave Law is passed with Southern support, toughening penalties for those aiding runaway slaves; slavery is banned in the District of Columbia; New Mexico and Utah are organized, with their inhabitants putting slavery to a popular vote.

1854
By the Kansas-Nebraska Act, inhabitants of newly organized territories will be allowed to vote on slavery; in reaction, politicians opposing the expansion of slavery found the Republican Party.

1857
The Supreme Court, in the *Dred Scott v. Sandford* decision, determines that African Americans, as property, cannot enjoy the rights of citizenship no matter where they live.

1860
Republican Abraham Lincoln is elected president; in December, South Carolina secedes from the Union, to be followed by ten additional Southern slaveholding states.

1861
The Civil War begins with the firing on Fort Sumter, a federal outpost in Charleston harbor.

1865
The Civil War ends with the defeat of the Confederacy; by the Thirteenth Amendment to the Constitution, slavery is banned throughout the United States.

For Further Research

Slave Narratives

William L. Andrews and Henry Louis Gates Jr., eds., *The Civitas Anthology of African American Slave Narratives.* Washington, DC: Civitas/Counterpoint, 1999.

Ira Berlin, Marc Favreau, and Steven F. Miller, eds., *Remembering Slavery: African Americans Talk About Their Personal Experience of Slavery and Freedom.* New York: New Press, 1998.

Robert J. Cottrol, *From African to Yankee: Narratives of Slavery and Freedom in Antebellum New England.* Armonk, NY: M.E. Sharpe, 1998.

Marie Diedrich, Henry Louis Gates Jr., and Carl Pedersen, eds., *Black Imagination and the Middle Passage.* New York: Oxford University Press, 1999.

General History of African Americans and Slavery

Paul Finkelman and Joseph C. Miller, eds., *Macmillan Encyclopedia of World Slavery.* New York: Macmillan Reference USA, Simon & Schuster, 1998.

John Hope Franklin, *From Slavery to Freedom: A History of African Americans.* New York: Alfred A. Knopf, 1994.

Nathan I. Huggins, Martin Kilson, and Daniel M. Fox, eds., *Key Issues in the Afro-American Experience.* New York: Harcourt Brace Jovanovich, 1971.

Peter Kolchin, *American Slavery, 1619–1877.* New York: Hill and Wang, 1993.

Randall M. Miller and John David Smith, eds., *Dictionary of Afro-American Slavery.* Westport, CT: Praeger, 1997.

Junius P. Rodriguez, ed., *The Historical Encyclopedia of World Slavery.* Santa Barbara, CA: ABC-CLIO, 1997.

Willie Lee Nichols Rose, *Slavery and Freedom.* New York: Oxford University Press, 1982.

Slavery in the Colonial Era

Ira Berlin, *Many Thousands Gone: The First Two Centuries of Slavery in North America.* Cambridge, MA: Belknap Press of Harvard University Press, 1998.

Patricia Bradley, *Slavery, Propaganda, and the American Revolution.* Jackson: University Press of Mississippi, 1998.

David Eltis, *The Rise of African Slavery in the Americas.* New York: Cambridge University Press, 2000.

Oscar Reiss, *Blacks in Colonial America.* Jefferson, NC: McFarland, 1997.

Slavery and the Antebellum South

Clement Eaton, *The Freedom-of-Thought Struggle in the Old South.* New York: Harper & Row, 1964.

John Hope Franklin, *Runaway Slaves: Rebels on the Plantation.* New York: Oxford University Press, 1999.

Robert Louis Paquette and Louis A. Ferleger, eds., *Slavery, Secession, and Southern History.* Charlottesville: University Press of Virginia, 2000.

Mark M. Smith, *Debating Slavery: Economy and Society in the Antebellum American South.* New York: Cambridge University Press, 1998.

Abolitionism, Secession, and the Civil War

Howard Jones, *Abraham Lincoln and a New Birth of Freedom: The Union and Slavery in the Diplomacy of the Civil War.* Lincoln: University of Nebraska Press, 1999.

Henry Mayer, *All on Fire: William Lloyd Garrison and the Abolition of Slavery.* New York: St. Martin's, 1998.

William Lee Miller, *Arguing About Slavery: The Great Battle in the United States Congress.* New York: Alfred A. Knopf, 1996.

Index